Straight
to the Top

Straight
to the Top

Becoming a
World-Class CIO

GREGORY S. SMITH

WILEY

John Wiley & Sons, Inc.

Copyright © 2006 by John Wiley & Sons, Inc. All rights reserved.

Published by John Wiley & Sons, Inc., Hoboken, New Jersey.

Published simultaneously in Canada.

For general information on our other products and services, or technical support, please contact our Customer Care Department within the United States at 800-762-2974, outside the United States at 317-572-3993 or fax 317-572-4002.

Wiley also publishes its books in a variety of electronic formats. Some content that appears in print may not be available in electronic books.

For more information about Wiley products, visit our Web site at http://www.wiley.com.

Library of Congress Cataloging-in-Publication Data:

Smith, Gregory S., 1963–
   Straight to the top : becoming a world-class CIO / Gregory S. Smith.
      p.   cm.
   Includes index.
   ISBN-13: 978-0-471-74478-8 (cloth)
   ISBN-10: 0-471-74478-6 (cloth)
   1. Chief information officers—Vocational guidance.   2. Information technology—Management—Vocational guidance.   3. Information resources management—Vocational guidance.   I. Title: Becoming a world-class chief information officer.   II. Title.
HD30.2.S629 2006
658.4'038—dc22

                                                              2006004007

Printed in the United States of America

10 9 8 7 6 5 4 3 2 1

To my family—Susanna, Anna, and Daniel—who have been wonderfully supportive and believe in me, regardless of what I attempt, and to Deborah Hechinger for making my first CIO experience exciting and challenging.

Contents

Preface

For the past five years, I have served as the vice president and chief information officer (CIO) of the World Wildlife Fund in Washington, DC. Prior to accepting my first CIO post and over the past decade, I have had the privilege of serving as a principal consultant for one of the most prestigious consulting firms in the world, as an IT director at a Fortune 200 financial services firm, and as an adjunct faculty member at a prestigious American university. Observations made and experiences gained over the past 20 years working in the information technology field have helped me to properly prepare for my first CIO role.

The role of the CIO in any organization is demanding and requires solid technical skills, business acumen, and exceptional communication skills to properly succeed. Preparing for the CIO role takes careful planning. Simply stated, this book is designed to help professionals aspiring to the role of the CIO to properly plan their career and give them guidance on the skills and knowledge that it takes to be a CIO today. Also, this book is designed to share with others my experience and planning that helped me land my first CIO role by the age of 37.

TARGET AUDIENCE

Straight to the Top: Becoming a World-Class CIO is targeted toward information technology and business professionals with aspirations of landing a senior management position in information technology or who desire to become a top IT resource in their organization. The book aims to communicate an effective *road map* and share experiences from leading CIO experts toward becoming a first-time CIO. Academic institutions that offer programs and degrees in information systems, computer science, and IT management and their faculty could benefit from this book by augmenting content in their courses to include real-world skills and a planning approach that can propel candidates to reach the upper echelon of technology management.

Tomorrow's successful technology professionals and leaders will be power users of technology, have a strong grasp on technology topics, and will integrate and work closely with other business executives and staff. *Straight to the Top* cuts to the chase and describes the key skills and relationships necessary to become the CIO. Readers will also get a view from the executive recruiter's perspective to see exactly what qualities, skills, and experiences quality search firms are seeking when searching for CIO candidates.

APPROACH

The information presented in this book along with recommendations come from a variety of sources: (1) advisory research and case studies, (2) interviews with a diverse range of CIO experts, (3) interviews with a variety of executive recruiting firms, (4) interviews with a select group of sales professionals, and (5) my own experiences in both planning for my first CIO role and serving as one in an internationally recognized conservation organization—the World Wildlife Fund. Expert CIOs surveyed for this book span a diverse group of organizations that include the following statistics and sectors:

- Average annual revenue of $1.3 billion, with the highest at $9.4 billion and the smallest at $40 million
- Industries/sectors: nonprofit, transportation, media, financial services, chemicals, legal, education, health care, real estate, construction, software services, and retail
- Geographical reach: 50 percent based in the domestic United States, 50 percent from international organizations

Part 1 focuses on the building blocks, including IT and communication skills needed to move up to midlevel technology management. Chapter 1 highlights the key skills that an aspiring CIO needs to have, such as networking fundamentals, application development and integration, database management systems, wireless technology, security, and Internet technologies. The importance of methodologies for technical and functional/process improvement and change management best practices are discussed, as is the need to comprehend IT governance structures and standards. Part 1 also includes a discussion about the importance of understanding business users and their needs, and how to build effective relationships outside of the IT *glass house*. In conclusion, this section of the book discusses the need for superior communication skills and how to translate *IT speak* into business terms.

Part 2 builds on the fundamentals discussed in the first half of the book and hones in on the key skills and experiences that employers and search firms are looking for when hiring a CIO. Readers will learn what top executive recruiters are looking for when hiring for senior IT leadership positions and how to build the skills required. This section will also discuss the importance of developing the right network that includes both IT and non-IT colleagues and the importance of sharing information and best practices within that network. Readers will also get exposed to some key skills and strategies for managing vendors and contracts as well as how to use sports to mix business with pleasure to get what you want as the senior IT buyer and consumer of technical goods and services in an organization. Part 2 also addresses the need for acquiring the right financial management skills and how to *think like a CFO* and *act like a CIO*. Finally, the book will conclude with a discussion on how to properly balance risks and rewards while moving up the IT ladder and what to expect once a candidate lands his or her first CIO position.

Acknowledgements

Over the past 20 years, I've had wonderful opportunities to learn, grow, and apply IT best practices to businesses and their customers. A number of folks were instrumental in my development. I am grateful to Barbara Sada for taking the time early in my career to mentor me on the importance of solid communications skills and effective presentation delivery. I'll never forget your advice; while seemingly simple, it is quite effective: *speak about what you know, know your audience, take time to prepare, and don't read from a script.* I'd like to thank my friend Michael Sheehan for his knowledge and guidance in the area of legal counsel, negotiation skills, and contract preparation and management. He was instrumental in the development of my contract negotiation and vendor relationship management skills. There are also a couple of special executives that taught me more about how to be successful by *their actions* instead of their words. A special thanks to two real role models: Vida Durant and Deborah Hechinger.

Also, a special thanks goes out to Stan Wakefield, who introduced me to the publishing team at John Wiley & Sons. I'd also like to thank the wonderful folks at *CIO* magazine, especially the CIO Executive Council staff, with special recognition to Carrie Mathews, Karen Fogerty, and Mark Hall for their help, research, and encouragement. In addition, I'd like to recognize and thank the kind folks at *eWeek*, especially my friends Eric Lundquist and Debra Donston, who I've had the pleasure to work with over the past decade on a variety of published articles and more recently as part of the *eWeek* Corporate Advisory Board.

Sound research is key to having a successful book. A special thanks to George Colony and the wonderful folks at Forrester Research Inc., which include Aaron Zarwan and contributing analysts, for providing me access to some of their vast research and trends database. I'd especially like to thank the expert CIOs who participated in the CIO survey and for their insight and recommendations that will likely help build the next generation of world-class CIOs. Another special thanks to all of the executive recruiting firms that gave great insight into what they and their customers are looking for in CIO candidates today. They include Martha Heller of the Z Resource Group, Katherine Graham of Heidrick & Struggles, Timothy Ward of the McCormick Group, Eric Sigurdson of Russell Reynolds Associates, and Beverly Lieberman of Halbrecht Lieberman Associates. I'd also like to thank Anne Topp from the World Wildlife Fund for her editorial review and feedback on the manuscript.

Special thanks also goes out to Bart Nagel for his creative photography and a really fun photo shoot. Also, in memory of Sondra Lundy Schaeffer, who encouraged me to be creative through publishing. She always shared my published works and articles with friends and was enthusiastic in her support. In closing, I'd like to pay special thanks to the wonderful folks at John Wiley & Sons, Inc., especially Timothy Burgard for his efforts in making this book a world-class publication. I'd also like to thank Sandy for those late night conversations when I was writing this text. Last, but not least, I'd like to thank my parents for their encouragement and support to invent and succeed. Dad, I wouldn't be where I am today if you hadn't convinced me to take up computer science in the early 1980s.

PART ONE

Building the Necessary
Skills and Relationships

CHAPTER 1

Key IT Skills to Have

Life is like a dog-sled team. If you ain't the lead dog, the scenery never changes.

—LEWIS GRIZZARD[1]

Before I jump into a discussion on why technology skills matter for technology executives today, I thought that it would be helpful to first clarify the difference between a chief information officer (CIO) and a chief technology officer (CTO) and provide a summary of both the recent evolution of the CIO role and the current state of the CIO profession.

THE CIO AND THE CTO—WHAT'S THE DIFFERENCE?

In general, the CIO is responsible for managing the information technology and investments that effectively align the use of technology with the goals of the business. Today, the CIO is a key executive in most organizations with oversight of the IT infrastructure, messaging systems, information assets, database repositories, and policies and procedures that ensure that the systems and information within are reliable, available, secure, and effective. The CTO, in contrast, has evolved as a right-hand technical executive, usually reporting directly to the CIO with oversight of designing and implementing complex technical solutions in support of the CIO's strategies and direction. The CTO is usually more concerned with *how* to implement complex solutions or products, is typically technically savvy, and is less experienced with dealing directly with the business units. In the late 1990s, the CTO title was the buzz among IT recruiters and CEOs. There were even mild predictions that the CTO role would rise up and become the lead IT executive position and cause the demise of the CIO as the shift toward a strategic focus for CIOs left a technical void at many organizations during the Internet boom. An executive search firm described the difference between the two CXO positions: "The CIO is 99.9 percent leadership, applying technology to solve business problems. The CTO focuses on technology more than strategy and vision."[2] Thus, the CTO to the rescue! According to a senior technology practice leader at Korn Ferry, the majority of IT executive job searches being conducted in May of 2000 were for a CTO with the majority of positions in startups and dot-coms.[3]

> It all started about a year and a half ago, when the rest of corporate America realized that the Amazon.com phenomenon was real and that the web had to be dealt with. Many CEOs just don't think that the CIO can handle it all—and so they are seeking CTOs to round out their IT leadership. What this says is that CIOs need to roll up their sleeves and start getting that Internet experience.[4]

The rise of the CTO typically came through one of a few paths in the 1990s. Organizations that produced technology products or services often hired a CTO to focus on product development and engineering. Also, firms that were large enough to support multiple IT executives carved out the CTO role to focus on *emerging technologies* and implement complex technical solutions, freeing CIOs to focus more of their attention on strategic issues associated with delivering solutions to the business units. In many companies today, the CIO and CTO work effectively together, usually with the CTO reporting directly to the CIO. In 2000, the CIO of CVS.com, who also worked with the CTO of CVS.com as well as the CIO of the parent CVS corporation, summed up the need for an external focus on customers, regardless of title:

> The world is changing. I know some CIOs who fear being replaced by CTOs. But the point is that you have to become more customer-centric— more externally focused—no matter what your title is, or else you will be pushed to the back office.[5]

Fast forward to today. What is the role of the CIO and CTO in companies today? The lines are sometimes blurred, but one thing is for sure—the CIO role is still the dominant IT leadership role in organizations, and the prophecy of the 1990s that the CTO would usurp the role of CIO has not been fulfilled. Some organizations have a CIO or CTO only, while others have both, but with clearly defined roles and separation of duties. According to a technology director quoted in a *Computing.com* article,

> There are definitely two functions occurring in technology. [One is] to make sure the business runs correctly, for the administration, control and management of information, [for which] you require a CIO. The CTO, on the other hand, should focus on technology development.[6]

The typical CTO has a background in IT, consulting, research and development, or engineering, an average head count of 47 IT staff, and 73 percent of CTOs work for smaller companies with $100 million or less in annual revenue.[7] In contrast, most CIOs have IT and consulting backgrounds, a larger IT staff (an average of 93), and 59 percent of them work for larger companies.[8] As far as titles go, the CTO title and role has yet to replace the CIO and take off in general. In the 2002 *CIO* magazine State of the CIO survey of 500 respondents, the majority (63 percent) of IT heads used the title of CIO, while only 13 percent indicated that their role and title was that of a CTO.[9]

The challenge for organizations today is to decide whether they need a CIO, CTO, both, or neither. In reality, many small to midsize organizations that are not engineering-based or product-centric will likely adopt a CIO as the top IT executive and usually can't afford multiple IT executives on the payroll. Larger organizations with ample IT budgets, diverse business offerings, higher levels of technology integration with suppliers and partners, and more complex requirements will likely continue to use both. Thus, it's often a hard sell for most companies to create a spot for the CTO unless there is a specific technical focus. However, there is usually great value for organizations that do carve out a niche for the more technical executive, as long as the role is complimentary to that of the CIO and there is synergy between the two.

There's plenty of room for multiple IT executives in today's complex business world as well as multiple paths to get there. One can take the traditional path of starting from an IT specialist/technician position, moving to line manager, and then eventually to the CIO as more supervisory responsibility kicks in along with additional tasks and projects that involve less direct technology involvement.[10] A health-care technology consulting firm CIO summed up the CTO career path:

> Now, with the creation of the CTO, a career path has emerged that precludes the dwindling of one's involvement with the technology. Whereas the line manager (IT manager) would move into the role of the CIO, the lead engineer is now well suited to assume the role of the CTO—the glue between the CIO and line management on technology issues.[11]

In conclusion, if a CIO is less technical and being asked to develop and deliver more complex engineering or product-based solutions, he or she should consider adding a CTO role to the organization. If the CIO serves in a more traditional organization that uses technology to meet demands of the business, then he or she should press ahead and take a seat at the IT throne and focus on delivery.

THE CHANGING ROLE OF THE CIO

The role of the CIO has evolved greatly over the past two decades. Large organizations have had CIOs for some time, but more small to midsize firms have recently created the new role for IT executives in their organizations. A recent *CIO* magazine article described the changing role of CIOs:

> In the early and late 1980s and early 1990s, the CIO position was much more tactical than strategic, and the CIO position was definitely more technical. [The executive committee] would tell you, "Don't worry— we'll figure out the strategic direction and you just make it run."[12]

Over the past 10 to 15 years, a few key technologies have had a direct impact on the shift toward strategic thinking for CIOs.

Client/Server Computing

The introduction and adoption of client/server computing in the 1980s and early 1990s combined with the rapid adoption of local area networks (LANs) pushed new technology and exciting graphical user interfaces (GUIs) into the hands of business users and consumers. This shift toward a decentralized computing model also increased the complexity of technology by having more components involved in system solutions supported by the IT staff and was a dramatic move away from the traditional centralized *IT glass house* model of hardware and services in the past. I often refer to this period in the evolution of computing models as the birth of *commoditized computing*, where access to business systems and information is made up of many different hardware devices (personal computers [PCs], file servers, centralized disk solutions, database servers, etc.), software components (local PC operating systems, browsers, application software, device drivers, etc.), and networking equipment (routers, firewalls, switches, etc.) interacting on a variety of levels.

The World Wide Web

Second was the birth of the World Wide Web (www) in the mid-1990s, which leveraged the client/server computing model and expanded it via the Internet. This shift toward Internet-enabled applications and information greatly expanded access to business customers via the web and radically changed the way that organizations thought about engaging with their customers and working with their vendors. This shift required most CIOs to change their planning approach from tactical, or short-range, to strategic with a longer planning outlook, typically three to five years. The shift in planning approach, along with new technologies and delivery mechanisms, improved the frequency of interaction with other senior members of the management team (see Exhibit 1.1) and resulted in a more *connected and engaged* CIO. Salem State's CIO defined strategic planning in 2002 as "trying to predict where an industry and business will be three to five years down the road and the technology that will get a company

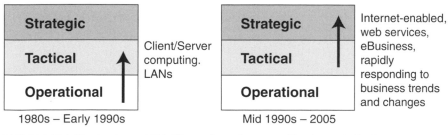

EXHIBIT 1.1   CIO Planning Focus—Past and Today

there."[13] Dell Inc. was one of the first companies to take advantage of the Internet boom and technologies by selling computers over the Internet. Their success in the direct-to-consumer sales approach has been copied by more companies in the last decade and has solidified Dell as one of the premier PC manufacturers in the world.

The Telecommmunications Boom

The third key technological advance to impact the role of the CIO was the telecommunications boom of the 1990s. The rapid expansion of companies and telecommunications technologies provided tremendous amounts of bandwidth to businesses via point-to-point private leased lines as well as increased capacity over the public Internet aided by the rapid growth of Internet service providers (ISPs). What followed shortly thereafter in the late 1990s was a rapid expansion of broadband access to the Internet for consumers. According to Forrester Research, U.S. business and residential digital subscriber lines (DSL) by major providers grew by more than 70 percent while cable modem subscribers increased 50 percent from 2000 to 2001.[14]

These three key technologies and capabilities had a dramatic impact on how the CIO interacts with other business lines and plans for growth strategies to support them and is likely to continue for the foreseeable future. According to a *CIO* magazine research article, successful CIOs in the early 1990s possessed four significant qualities: (1) They were vision builders who could deliver results or gain a competitive advantage via the use of technology; (2) they were good relationship builders; (3) they had sound tactical judgment and knew to not plan too far ahead of the business; and (4) they had the ability to detect when a change in business direction would impact IT.[15] Today's CIOs, however, will also have to adapt to the rapidly changing business environment. They'll need to understand the business, be technically savvy, have excellent communications skills, and think strategically and deliver operationally. *CIO* magazine sums up the transition nicely:

> The era of the information superhighways and e-commerce has changed the business perception of the importance of IT. Some executives see in it both business threats and opportunities, so IT has to define what systems are needed to support business strategy and how IT might change

it. CIOs are being asked to be *strategists*. There's never been a more exciting time to be a CIO. Hardly anybody in business doubts that we've
entered the information age and that IT is driving it. And once business-
people realize that technology needs to be scalable, diversifiable and
robust, they will know they need professional help. This is perhaps the
biggest opportunity that's come along for CIOs to show they're business
strategists.[16]

STATE OF THE CIO

Today's CIOs are predominantly men (87 percent) and more experienced
in a variety of skills beyond just core technology.[17] Information technology
backgrounds tend to be the primary background for CIOs today, but a
great many of them also have experience in consulting, business operations,
administration, and finance. According to a *CIO* magazine State of the CIO
2004 survey, nearly 70 percent of CIOs have information technology as
the primary job experience background, trailed by 7 percent for consulting,
7 percent business operations (non-IT), 5 percent finance and accounting,
2 percent administration, and 1 percent engineering[18] (see Exhibit 1.2).

Additional non-IT job experience includes consulting (62 percent), business operations (45 percent), administration (34 percent), customer service

IT	70%
Consulting	7%
Business operations (not IT operations)	7%
Finance/Accounting	5%
Administration	2%
Engineering	1%
Manufacturing/ Production	1%
Marketing	1%
Sales	1%
Other	3%

NOTE: There were no responses for customer service,
logistics or R&D.

EXHIBIT 1.2   **Primary Job Experience in Your Career**
Source: Adapted from "State of the CIO 2004," *CIO* magazine, October 1, 2004.

(26 percent), engineering (25 percent), finance and accounting (24 percent), and sales (21 percent).[19] Thus, today's CIOs needs to be more savvy about other facets of the business than just technology. Preparation for such a responsibility should not be taken lightly and needs to be carefully planned out and coordinated.

A *CIO* magazine 2004 survey also reported that the majority of CIOs carry the title of just CIO or CIO and vice president.[20] A recent Forrester Research report that surveyed 1,300 technology decision makers indicated that the approximately 50 percent of CIOs in North America and Europe reported to either the CEO, chief operating officer (COO) or president, while 27 percent reported directly to the CFO.[21] Larger organizations typically have a higher percentage of CIOs reporting to the CEO than smaller ones.[22] Interestingly, companies in the survey where the CIO reported directly to the CFO had the lowest percentage (3.3 percent) of their annual revenue spent on IT [23] (see Exhibits 1.3 and 1.4).

There is a lot of pressure on today's CIOs to innovate in support of their businesses and to help drive new product development, increase operational efficiencies, and deliver clear and measurable results. According to the *CIO* magazine State of the CI05 survey of 85 *global* CIOs, the majority (42 percent) of respondents indicated that they along with their business leaders and other CXOs are accountable for innovation results.[24] In addition, 65 percent of the CIOs surveyed indicated that bringing ideas for IT-enabled *business innovation* was a significant function of their role as the

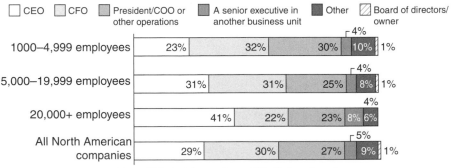

Base: 775 decision-makers at North American firms

EXHIBIT   1.3   **Who does the CIO, or senior-most IT decision-maker, report to?**

Source: Adapted from "Where Should the CIO Report," Forrester Research Inc., February 28, 2005.

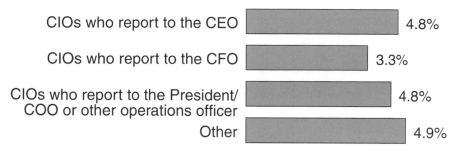

CIOs who report to the CEO   4.8%

CIOs who report to the CFO   3.3%

CIOs who report to the President/
COO or other operations officer   4.8%

Other   4.9%

EXHIBIT 1.4   **What Percentage of Your Company's Revenue is Spent on IT?**

Source: Adapted from "Where Should the CIO Report," Forrester Research Inc., February 28, 2005.

IT executive.[25] So who are the main beneficiaries of IT-led innovation and what are the goals? According to the *CIO* magazine survey, customer service (70 percent), administration and finance (51 percent), sales and marketing (42 percent), and IT operations (39 percent) round out the top four business beneficiaries, whereas the top three goals of innovation were reported as reducing costs/improving productivity (81 percent), improving customer satisfaction (71 percent), and creating a competitive advantage (66 percent).[26] Thus, today's CIO must integrate well with other CXOs and understand the business needs in order to be able to lead IT-enabled innovation to help them.

HOW IMPORTANT ARE CORE TECHNOLOGY SKILLS?

Are solid IT skills important today to be successful as a CIO? Absolutely! Most of the research out in the market today, however, indicates that technology skills for CIOs ranks at a much lower priority and that business acumen and communication skills are at the top of the list of *must have* skills. Many CIOs that I've spoken with over the years and encountered via peer meetings and conference calls do not appear to have sufficient knowledge of information technology and appear to rely heavily on their trusted subordinates to give them advice and help them make the right decisions. This can be a dangerous road, because these subordinates will in many ways determine how successful the CIO is. As a CIO, I can't imagine leading a team of IT professionals without solid technical skills. Today's CIOs need to have core technology skills in addition to many other soft skills; they need to be the *whole package*. The days are gone when IT leaders are just IT experts or from other non-IT disciplines running the IT department. CIOs today can't properly lead a technical staff and department if they don't have solid technical knowledge—bottom line. Would you trust and follow a CFO that didn't have a strong financial and accounting background? Then why should companies settle for CIOs that don't have a solid grasp of IT fundamentals? The following sections take a look at some recent research and discuss how several world-class CIOs view the importance of technology skills and how to obtain them.

Key IT Skills and Knowledge for CIOs Today

In a recent *CIO* magazine research poll of 400 IT professionals (see Exhibit 1.5), slightly over half of the survey respondents (55 percent) believed that their CIOs have an appropriate understanding of the company's current technology.[27] While the numbers seem flattering on the surface, they are just over 50 percent, revealing that as many as 45 percent of IT staffers believe that their CIOs are not technically savvy. In the same survey, IT staffers indicated that their CIOs were doing a good job setting IT strategy and steering the IT organization, but fell short on staff development and were out of touch with stress levels and morale in their department.[28]

What do practicing CIOs think are important IT skills and backgrounds to have today? As part of the research for this book, I surveyed a diverse group of CIOs on a variety of topics. The survey results and quotes that follow throughout the book under the heading of "CIO Survey Question" are their answers, insights, and recommendations.

Given today's complex systems, interfaces, and the continuing need to

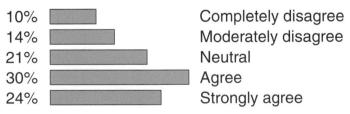

10%	Completely disagree
14%	Moderately disagree
21%	Neutral
30%	Agree
24%	Strongly agree

EXHIBIT 1.5   **IT Staff Survey: My CIO Has an Appropriate Understanding of the Company's Current Technology**

Source: Adapted from "What Do You Think of Your CIO," *CIO Research Reports*, September 15, 2003.

What are the most important *IT skills/knowledge* needed for a CIO position today?

- The most common response was for the need to have general technology skills. Knowledge of IT architectures was also important.
- Coming in second was the ability to translate business and IT needs into an easy-to-understand IT vision and strategy.

What technology areas do you rely on subordinates the most for guidance and recommendations?" In other words, which technology topics are you weakest in?

- 60 percent responded with architecture and infrastructure.
- 25 percent indicated systems management.
- 25 percent responded with security and/or regulations.

show the value of IT, my personal experience as well as my research indicates that it is paramount for CIOs to have a solid understanding of the following:

- Applications and architecture alternatives
- Database management systems
- Networking concepts and wireless technologies
- Security

Applications, whether developed internally or purchased from a vendor as a COTS (commercial off-the-shelf) solution, bring IT staff closest to the business units since they must understand their requirements in order to implement a solution. At the World Wildlife Fund (WWF), our donor enterprise resource planning (ERP) system brings together IT, development, marketing, and finance professionals to build a cohesive and integrated team that is focused on getting results. To properly provide support for enterprise applications, the IT team and CIO need to understand these applications, integration between related applications, and the variety of technical architecture choices that they run on to properly deploy and deliver reliable system solutions. Today's inventory of applications used in businesses are large, with many purchased directly from vendors, while others may be custom developed to meet specific needs not usually met with commercial software or to gain a competitive advantage. Either way, software applications are the heart of most organizations. Today's applications can reside on something as simple as a networked computer or PC, to a complex and integrated set of servers and software combinations that can include many different options, including terminal emulation, client/ server or two-tier computing, n-tier application server technology, and load balanced web-based solutions. While most CIOs rely heavily on IT architects and network professionals for the bulk of these architecture options, they still need to understand the basic technologies along with the pros and cons of each architecture option before deciding on a solution and set of IT standards. Several powerful and new technologies like Java applications, Java J2EE application services, web services, and service-oriented architectures (SOA) are adding additional IT complexity, while providing the framework for scalable and reliable architectures for the future. CIOs need to spend time with their staff and vendors to properly understand these technologies. Once understood, CIOs can begin to develop IT standards to help lower overall costs, limit the number of diverse technologies in their organization, and build an effective support organization with the right set of skills to support it.

Database management systems are usually at the heart of most applications and store the organization's gold—both raw data and meaningful information. Almost every organization has a database and application package that stores the following information: human resource information system (HRIS), financial expense and revenue, customer relationship management (CRM), and budgeting. There are a number of commercial database offerings on the market today to choose from, including free or near-free solutions from Postgress SQL and MySQL, midpriced solutions from Microsoft SQLServer, to more expensive offerings from Oracle, Informix, and DB2. Database technology today is both mature and robust, but still requires the right skills to manage and administer the database repositories, which is usually left to database administrators (DBAs). However, CIOs today who understand the fundamentals of database technology can use it to their advantage in a number of ways. They can provide guidance and standards to their staff in the selection and standardization on one or more products as well as help drive operating efficiencies by integrating different data throughout the organization via *smart* online database links and interfaces. Business users are continually looking to IT to present different views and reports of their organization's data. All of this information usually sits in one or more databases in an organization. Putting in place the right architecture is key to being able to capture data entry and provide for efficient and timely analysis and reporting to key decision makers (see Exhibit 1.6). Thus, CIOs need to pay attention to this function of their organization and get up to speed. Don't forget, the "I" in the CIO title is synonymous with the *information* that resides in most corporate databases.

Networking concepts and wireless technologies are important to understand since these are the mediums in which all application access and database content is delivered to users. Key topics to understand in this area include networking protocols and topologies, evaluating vendor solutions and equipment, telecommunication and bandwidth options for site

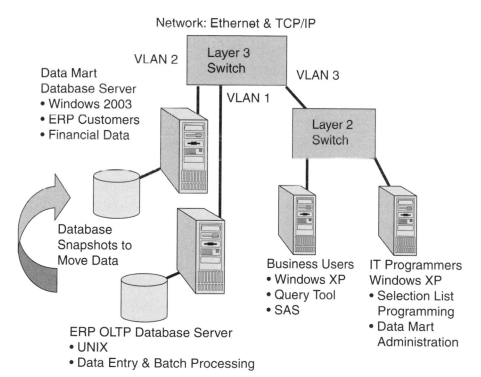

EXHIBIT 1.6   **Sample IT Online Transaction Processing (OLTP) to Decision Support Architecture**

interconnectivity, voice-over Internet protocol (VOIP), storage and backup solutions, and wireless technologies. The networking professionals that support this area usually run the infrastructure for their organization and are highly relied upon by the CIO for delivery of content and information throughout the organization. However, the CIO needs to be engaged with the networking folks in the IT department in order to make key decisions on IT standards, vendor products, solutions, and security. Without an understanding of the applications and the network on which they ride, the CIO can't possibly be effective as a business partner and IT leader for which to deliver services and information.

VOIP is a networking-related technology that CIOs need to be up on today, since it offers the capability of delivering high-quality voice conversations over data networks, thus integrating typically diverse technologies (voice and data) over a single medium. While the market is still emerging and technology standards are evolving, VOIP promises to be one of the more interesting technology areas to watch in the coming years that will likely have a dramatic impact on how organizations communicate within offices and to remote locations, potentially across the globe. WWF is currently experimenting with VOIP over the public Internet in an effort to use the technology to expand our voice capacity to our international field offices, while dramatically lowering costs.

Wireless networks and applications are exploding across the globe and forcing IT professionals to keep pace in order to provide timely and wire-free access to systems and information. The adoption of wireless technology by consumers and business is a foregone conclusion and fact. Millions of people are using the technology to stay connected to their systems, friends, and family wherever they are. According to ABI, a technology research firm in Oyster Bay, New York, that was recently quoted in a *New York Times* article: "More than 10 million homes in the United States now have a Wi-Fi base station providing a wireless Internet connection. There were essentially none as recently as 2000."[29] Road warrior business travelers are also demanding wireless technologies including always-on personal digital assistants (PDAs) to keep pace in a competitive environment. Businesses are using wireless fidelity (WiFi) and other wireless technologies as a method of staying connected with their customers. Worldwide interoperability for microwave access (WiMax), with signal ranges of up to 30 miles, is on the near horizon and will likely usher in the next wave of affordable wireless Internet access among businesses and consumers. In short, wireless technologies are here to stay, and CIOs need to get up to speed quickly, while understanding the risks associated with them in order to provide secure solutions and protect their systems and information.

Security is the final area that CIOs need to pay particular attention to today. There are many threats, externally and internally, that can put an organization's data and systems at risk today. IT organizations around the globe are spending enormous amounts of money to protect their data and networks from prying eyes. Areas of focus in this category include intrusion detection and prevention, anti-virus, anti-spyware, anti-SPAM, database and information security, and network security. If the data network is impacted in a negative way that prevents business customers from accessing their applications and data, the CIO will usually hear about it quickly. Bottom line, the CIO is accountable for system availability and data security. CIOs today can no longer just rely on network professionals, the chief security officer (CSO), or outsource providers to secure their systems and information. They must take an active role in establishing a security presence within their IT organization and take the time to work with the various professionals to understand the risks, review options for mitigating them, and make the final call on how to protect against the threats. According to a recent *CIO* magazine research survey of IT professionals, less than half of them believe that CIOs are paying enough attention to security issues.[30]

On March 5, 2005, the *Washington Post* reported that ChoicePoint Inc., one of the largest information services vendors in the United States, fell victim to an identity theft scam that resulted in the theft of confidential data for 145,000 people.[31] Ten days later, the *Washington Post* reported that identity thieves had penetrated LexisNexis, a world-wide provider of legal and business data, and that 32,000 consumers were affected.[32] The *Wall Street Journal* followed up with an article in May 2005 that ChoicePoint was struggling with how to identify which records were stolen. Lieutenant Robert Costa, head of the Los Angeles County Sheriff's office, said "They [ChoicePoint] said it was a huge task and they didn't have the staff to do it."[33] Lieutenant Costa continued that "apparently their technology wasn't built so you were able to find the electronic footsteps these guys left."[34]

Worrisome indeed, but bottom line—CIOs that don't pay attention to system security run the risk of getting their systems hacked or information compromised, lost, or stolen. At the end of the day, the CIO is accountable and his or her job may be on the line.

Finally, disaster recovery (DR) planning falls into this chapter since it encompasses several key IT skills to have, while planning for the *right* recovery solution. CIOs must appropriately plan to preserve their organization's data, develop a recovery model and plan that works for their budget and organizational risk profile, build a solution, and test it. The DR plan includes *application* recovery, including *database* management content, *network* design to ensure delivery of content, and *secure infrastructures* to ward off external and internal threats. Thus, the DR plan is essentially the recovery capacity and risk mitigation strategy of an organization's key systems and information assets that are usually owned by key business units and made up of the key areas of skills that I believe CIOs need to have to properly lead an IT team of professionals effectively and with respect.

Follow the Money . . .

A Robert Half Technology poll of more than 1,400 CIOs in 2005 found that IT spending in the next 12 months would focus on network security (35 percent), database upgrade/installation (16 percent), CRM systems (15 percent), data storage and backup (13 percent), and wireless communications (10 percent).[35] A February 2005 *CIO* magazine Tech Poll of 231 respondents revealed that the top three technology categories expecting an increase in spending were security software (58 percent), storage systems (53.9 percent), and computer hardware (48.9 percent), with an anticipated increase in spending also in the area of data networking equipment (44.2 percent).[36] Increased spending is often tied to hiring additional IT professionals. A recent article on IntranetJournal.com indicated that high-tech security professionals looking for jobs are in a good position going forward and that network security, intrusion detection, and penetration tests will be big for organizations in 2005.[37] Jeff Markham, branch manager for Robert Half Technology, summed up the network security risk and opportunity: "This was the biggest year ever for viruses and SPAM. A lot of the way we define security is on the database side—securing confidential information like credit card numbers and the personal information of customers."[38]

Additional trends in IT spending point to a focus on areas that include applications development, database management systems, and networking. A recent Forrester Research report on IT spending found that IT spending by companies in the United States in 2005 will grow on average at 7 percent annually.[39] Specific areas for annual growth include computer hardware (9 percent), network and communications equipment slows after a flurry of purchasing in 2004 (4 percent), software grows slightly (5 percent), with a solid focus on systems management, storage software, custom built applications (19 percent), and security applications leading the way.[40] European Enterprise spending in 2005 is forecasted to trail the United States with an expected spending increase of 2.9 percent, with a strong interest in VOIP, VPN, security spending, and business intelligence platforms and applications.[41]

According to the *CIO* magazine State of the CIO5 survey, respondents indicated that the top technologies for innovation were redesigning IT architectures (73 percent), data access/warehousing (55 percent), and web services (49 percent).[42] From a global CIO priority perspective, CIOs in the United States, Japan, South Korea, Southeast Asia, Germany, Australia, and Canada indicated that the top three technical priorities in 2005 were to integrate/enhance systems and processes, ensure data security and integrity, and focus on external customer service and relationship management.[43] In conclusion, CIOs will likely spend time staying current and abreast of the technologies that they are spending the most money on. Candidates aspiring to the role of the CIO should take notice of this trend and start developing the core technology skills now, while paying attention to what is on the current and future IT horizon.

Remaining Current on Key Technologies

Once a solid base of knowledge is established, remaining current on technology can be a challenge given the rapid pace of technological change and the lack of time to absorb key information. Most CIOs today employ a combination of efforts to remain current on the *right* technologies. Below are results from a recent CIO survey that asked a group of world-class CIOs how they stay current.

As a CIO, how do you remain current on technologies that are important today in the marketplace?
The highest response was via reading publications and subscriptions. The second highest was by attending conferences and seminars. The third highest was by vendor demos, meetings, and reading product white papers. The fourth highest was by interacting with internal IT staff. The fifth highest was peer visits and conference calls via established networks.

What's the Best Academic and Experience Background?

I believe that investing in an academic background to launch your career is paramount. Given the high cost of an education, it may turn out to be one of the most important decisions that a person can make regarding his or her career. Competition for top IT jobs is tough and competitive. A degree alone will not ensure your rise to the top, but the *right degrees* may just give a candidate the necessary edge. In a recent *TechRepublic* article, two leading experts summarized the right CIO background as follows:

> The duties of today's CIOs require a skill set that includes both a strong business background and a core technical background, such as a degree in computer science or another technology-oriented discipline. However, a CIO is not (or should not be) the lead engineer or programmer.[44]

I asked a group of leading CIOs the following question to find out just how important an academic background is in today's environment.

Is an academic background important for ascending to the role of the CIO today?
- 70 percent responded yes
- 20 percent responded no.
- 10 percent provided no response.

Several CIOs in the survey added their comments and advice below:

A formal education is neither a ticket for success nor a showstopper if you don't have a degree. It is not causative, but it appears to be coincidental that my most capable/deepest up 'n' comers also have the best degrees from the best universities.

—John W. Von Stein, Executive Vice President
and CIO, The Options Clearing House,
CIO magazine CIO Executive Council Member

Yes, mostly as a price of entry. It provides an unproven entity with poker chips for admittance to the game.

—Martin Gomberg, CTO, A&E Television Networks,
CIO magazine CIO Executive Council Member

There are several options for professionals today to add knowledge and skills, ranging from undergraduate degrees to IT certifications to advanced graduate degrees. Which degrees are the most helpful in grooming for the CIO slot? Many universities and colleges have started to adapt to the rapidly changing business world that is so reliant on technology by creating programs that are designed to combine business and IT skills into a single program. Many colleges and universities offer advanced masters degrees with titles like an "MS in Business" or a "technical MBA." One thing for sure is that IT skills alone won't typically get you the CIO role. According to a *Computerworld* article titled "Masters in Frustration," the dean of Boston University's School of Management, which offers a dual-degree graduate program called the MS-MBA, summed up the need for a new program: "The next generation of CEOs is coming from IT, not from finance. What business problem do you know that isn't being solved by technology?"[45]

Again, I asked a distinguished group of CIOs for their feedback.

CIO SURVEY

What degree(s) would you recommend to professionals wanting to become a CIO and why?

Having a computer science background is a must for progressive CIOs to ensure that basic knowledge of what they are managing and responsible for is there. Additionally, it is beneficial to understand

and/or have a formal education in business management/finance to tie the benefits of technology to the business needs.

—Shyam K. Dunna, CIO/Assistant General Manager,
MARTA (Metropolitan Atlanta Rapid Transit Authority),
CIO magazine CIO Executive Council Member

Having an MBA provides a basis and background in the key components of business and the things that CXO types focus on, including finances, operations, legal issues, market positioning, etc. An MBA gives you more information about how technology can directly and positively affect the business. From a credibility perspective, having an MBA makes you more "equal" with other senior executives, as they often have an MBA degree as well.

—Steven W. Agnoli, CIO, Kirkpatrick & Lockhart Nicholson
Graham LLP, CIO magazine CIO Executive Council Member

In your opinion, what background (IT, administration, sales, accounting, etc.) is ideal for a candidate wanting to ascend to the role of the CIO today?

According to the 2004 State of the CIO by *CIO* magazine:

- 70 percent of the 544 CIO respondents indicated that their primary background was in IT.
- 45 percent said that they had also worked in business operations (45 percent), administration (34 percent), finance or accounting (24 percent), and sales (21 percent).[46]

Highlighted quotes from other CIOs are below.

I firmly believe that having a background in IT is essential for a CIO. While it is very important for CIOs to interact with the business for process improvement and optimization, underlying this is an infrastructure that supports these applications that drive business growth. We must, first and foremost, deliver applications and services to our internal and external customers in a secure and reliable fashion or we put ourselves and our organization at risk. To attempt this without a solid background in technology is not a risk I would be willing to take.

—Hans Keller, CTO, National Aquarium in Baltimore,
CIO magazine CIO Executive Council Member

I would strongly recommend an IT background for anyone wanting to be a CIO. Developing the IT skills early in a career and gaining experience in other parts of a business throughout the career might be a pathway to success.

—Jerry B. Hale, CIO and Vice President of Information
Technology, Eastman Chemical Company, CIO *magazine*
CIO Executive Council Member

WHAT DID I DO TO PREPARE?

I started out my career by obtaining an undergraduate degree in computer science with a minor in business. After working several years as a programmer in a consulting firm, where I proactively shared knowledge with co-workers and worked toward being part of a team effort, I became a team leader, which gave me oversight over larger projects and consulting engagements. I enrolled in a graduate "technical MBA" degree program with a concentration on technology management to expand my business knowledge and gain additional skills for IT oversight and management. In the early 1990s, I moved to a large financial services Fortune 200 firm to expand my skills and work with larger, more complex systems, including financial systems, real-time trading applications, complex telecommunications delivery systems (terrestrial and satellite for financial feeds), Internet-enabled applications, database management systems, and decision support/business intelligence systems. In 1992, at the age of 29, I published my first article in *LAN Times,* which highlighted how to integrate Novell and Banyan Vines networks. This was the exciting start of my publishing aspirations.

RECOMMENDATIONS

To close this chapter out, I advise professionals aspiring to become CIOs to not lose focus on the core technology skills that are necessary to run a world-class IT shop. Individuals today are more in charge of their career and planning than ever before. Planning your career earlier, while setting clear, measured, and obtainable goals, can get you to where you want to be if you are persistent and patient. The following recommendations are designed to help candidates prepare for an IT leadership role:

- Pursue educational degrees to compliment your background and strengthen your IT and business knowledge.
- Pursue certification programs that add hot IT skills and knowledge.
- Get some consulting experience. Consulting engagements offer a unique way to learn what businesses need and how to deliver value from an entirely different perspective.
- Map out a training plan to fill technology and business gaps and work with your supervisor to make it happen.
- Get engaged with vendors that you do business with (or may in the future) to learn new technologies and/or processes that can be applied to today's complex business challenges.
- Conduct brown bag sessions for training and information sharing of technology and business topics within your department and other IT staff and encourage others to do the same.
- Volunteer to join project teams where you can gain additional IT skills and business knowledge.
- Attend free vendor information and demo sessions on relevant technology topics.
- Read periodicals and publications to gain additional insights and perspectives.
- Get involved with the DR team and participate in a recovery test, which focuses on restoring mission critical applications, databases, networks, and security devices.
- Conduct research, where applicable, and review *best practices* and vendor solutions needed to solve real business problems.
- Start developing your peer network now to share ideas and best practices.

In closing, a CIO that has strong technical skills adds tremendous value to an organization and their technical staff by clearly understanding the interworkings, costs, and benefits of different technology solutions that enable them to more rapidly map the best strategy for solving technical and business challenges for their organization and business customers.

ENDNOTES

1. Lewis Grizzard, *The Wit and Wisdom of Lewis Grizzard* (Marietta, GA: Longstreet Press, 1995), cover page.

2. Lorraine Cosgrove Ware, "Trendlines: Whatever Happened to the CTO," *CIO* magazine (August 1, 2002), www.cio.com/archive/080102/tl_role_content.html (accessed March 14, 2005).

3. Mindy Blodgett, "The Wolf at the Door," *CIO* magazine (May 15, 2000), www.cio.com/archive/051500/cover.html (accessed March 14, 2005).

4. Ibid.

5. Ibid.

6. Miya Knights, "CIO and CTO Roles Diverge," *IT Week* (March 8, 2004), www.computing.co.uk/print/it/1153320 (accessed March 16, 2005).

7. Ware, "Trendlines: Whatever Happened to the CTO."

8. Ibid.

9. Edward Prewitt, "The State of the CIO," *CIO* magazine (March 1, 2002), www.cio.com/archive/030102/survey_results.html (accessed March 25, 2005).

10. Scott P. Mullins and Jason R. Klinowski, "Defining the Complementary Job Roles of the CTO and CIO," Builder.com (April 18, 2003), www.builder.com/ 5102-6401-5034729.html (accessed March 16, 2005).

11. Ibid.

12. Erik Berkman, "Skills—Successful CIOs Stress Business Acumen, Not Technical Expertise," *CIO* magazine (March 1, 2002), www.cio.com/archive/030102/skills .html (accessed February 17, 2005).

13. Ibid.

14. Lisa Pierce, "US DSL and Cable Modem Forecast for 2002–2005" (May 21, 2002) (Cambridge, MA: Forrester Research), www.forrester.com/Research/ LegacyIT/0,7208,27652,00.html (accessed March 16, 2005).

15. Edward Prewitt and Stephanie Overby, *Fundamentals of the CIO Role—The Evolution of the CIO Role* (Framingham, MA: CXO Media, 2003), 6.

16. Ibid., 8.

17. Edward Prewitt and Lorraine Cosgrove Ware, "State of the CIO 2004: The Survey," *CIO* magazine, (October 1, 2004), www.cio.com/archive/100104/survey .html (accessed February 17, 2005.

18. Ibid.

19. Ibid.

20. Ibid.

21. Marc Cecere and Heather Liddell, "Where Should the CIO Report?" (February 28, 2005) (Cambridge, MA: Forrester Research), www.forrester.com/Research/ Document/0,7211,36314,00.html (accessed March 5, 2005).

22. Ibid.

23. Ibid.

24. Elana Varon and Lorraine Cosgrove Ware, "The State of the CIO Around the World," *CIO* magazine (May 1, 2005), http://www2.cio.com/research/surveyreport.cfm?id=87 (accessed December 5, 2005).

25. Ibid.

26. Ibid.

27. Lorraine Cosgrove Ware, "What Do You Think of Your CIO?" *CIO Research Reports* (September 15, 2003), http://www2.cio.com/research/surveyreport.cfm?id=63 (accessed February 26, 2005).

28. Ibid.

29. Seth Schiesel, "Growth of Wireless Internet Opens New Paths for Thieves," *New York Times,* March 19, 2005, www.nytimes.com/2005/03/19/technology/19wifi.html (accessed March 25, 2005).

30. Ware, "What Do You Think of Your CIO?"

31. Robert O'Harrow Jr., "ChoicePoint Data Cache Became a Powder Keg," *Washington Post,* March 5, 2005, A01.

32. Jonathan Krim and Robert O'Harrow Jr., "Data Under Siege," *The Washington Post,* March 10, 2005, E01.

33. Evan Perez and Rick Brooks, "For Big Vendor of Personal Data, A Theft Lays Bare the Downside," *Wall Street Journal,* May 3, 2005, 1.

34. Ibid.

35. "Safety First," Robert Half Technology, online press release web site (February 25, 2005), www.roberthalftechnology.com/PressRoom (accessed February 27, 2005).

36. "IT Spending Projections Rebound Slightly in February," *CIO* magazine, (March 1, 2005), Tech Poll web site, peoplepolls.com/TechPollFebUE.pdf (accessed March 27, 2005).

37. Michael Pastore, "Security the Hot Spot for IT Jobs in 2005," *Intranet Journal* (January 1, 2005), www.intranetjournal.com/articles/200501/pij_01_18_05a.html (accessed February 27, 2005).

38. Ibid.

39. Andrew Bartels, *North American IT Spending in 2005* (November 19, 2004) (Cambridge, MA: Forrester Research, Inc.), www.forrester.com/Research/Print/Document/0,7211,35063,00.html (accessed March 15, 2005).

40. Ibid.

41. Manuel Angel Mendez, "2005 IT Spending: European Enterprises" (December 21, 2004) (Cambridge, MA: Forrester Research), www.forrester.com/Research/Print/Document/0,7211,35384,00.html (accessed March 5, 2005).

42. Varon and Ware, "The State of the CIO Around the World."

43. Ibid.

44. Mullins and Klinowski, "Defining the Complementary Job Roles of the CTO and CIO."

45. Don Tennant, "Masters of Frustration," *Computer World* (February 21, 2005), www.computerworld.com/printthis/2005/0,4814,99866,00.html (accessed March 22, 2005).

46. Edward Prewitt, "The CIO Role Ranges Beyond IT," *CIO* magazine (November 1, 2004), www.cio.com/archive/110104/hs_reports.html (accessed February 17, 2005).

CHAPTER 2

Methodologies, Projects, and IT Change Management

So much of what we call management consists in making it difficult for people to work.

—PETER DRUCKER[1]

Methodologies, project management, and IT change management are three *key* interrelated tools (see Exhibit 2.1) that IT professionals should be using to successfully manage technology today. As the introductory quote by Peter Drucker suggests, many outside of the IT discipline often feel that these tools simply add time, more work, and documentation to projects. The reality is that they do, but the pros strongly outweigh the cons for adopting their use. These tools, if used properly, can empower an IT organization to partner with their business units and achieve better results and accuracy associated with the implementation of mid- to large-scale projects. This chapter will present an overview of each topic and discuss why these tools are important in today's complex IT environment.

WHAT ARE METHODOLOGIES AND WHY ARE THEY IMPORTANT?

Webster's dictionary defines a method as "a way of doing anything; mode; procedure; process; esp., a regular, orderly, definite procedure or way of

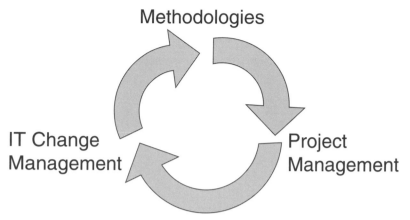

EXHIBIT 2.1   Frameworks, Plans, and Managing IT Change

teaching, investigating, etc."[2] Today methodologies are used on some of the simplest tasks to the most complex systems installations and implementations. Something as simple as cutting the lawn employs the fundamentals of methodologies. I've watched a neighbor of mine for years now follow the same process in cutting his yard:

1. Put gas into the mower

2. Start the mower

3. Trim around all the trees first, starting with the front yard and moving to the back

4. Resume mowing in the front yard, starting at the mailbox and cutting parallel to the sidewalk, moving back and forth closer to the house with each pass until completed

5. Edge the lawn starting with the driveway before moving down the sidewalk, and finally

6. Place the lawn bags full of fresh grass clippings in the same exact spot near the entrance to his garage.

As a result of watching this repeatable behavior, I have forced myself to follow a different path from time to time when cutting my own yard, which affords me the opportunity to see my own property from a different angle and perspective.

In business, methodologies are often used in system implementations that involve or are owned by the business units as well as larger IT infrastructure projects that don't have a formal business sponsor. A formal methodology is essentially a framework and set of defined processes and procedures for accomplishing a set of tasks, some of which are highly complex and time consuming. Many large consulting firms and vendors use them for complex client system installations and implementations as part of their consulting engagements. The larger vendor-independent consulting firms—specifically PricewaterhouseCoopers, Ernst & Young, Deloitte Touche Tohmatsu, and Bearing Point—have developed comprehensive methodologies, use them religiously, and are the de facto industry experts. Consulting firms typically employ methodologies for just about anything, ranging from process improvement, business change management, auditing, and system implementation engagements. Methodologies have many benefits (see Exhibit 2.2), most notably the use of defined and repeatable processes to identify business system requirements and implement solutions on time and at or under budget. In addition, they help create a structure of accountability for projects, by ensuring that deliverable products at various phases are agreed upon and signed off. One of the most common mistakes

EXHIBIT 2.2   METHODOLOGY/TECHNICAL FRAMEWORK BENEFITS

Creates structure and accountability for technical project implementations

Focuses on business and/or operational benefits to the organization
Contains defined steps and deliverables
Requires signatory approvals in both the business unit and IT
Team organizational structure maximizes resources and expertise and places shared responsibility in the appropriate business units

Uses repeatable processes and procedures

Minimizes errors in implementation by focusing up front on business and technical requirements
Produces better project results and lowers costs
Prevents against scope creep
Usually produces higher-quality products and deliverables
Gains credibility with business units
Provides for consistent project documentation

made today in implementing systems is a lack of detail for documenting requirements combined with a lack of ownership from the business unit for the final solution. Methodologies combined with the right project organizational structure can mitigate these risks if used properly and build a comprehensive and productive team made up of both IT and business professionals in search of common goals and objectives.

Most methodologies use defined *routes* or *maps* along with multiple *phases* with detailed instructions and *tasks* that are to be completed in order to properly complete each phase. Routes may be used to identify the different types of system implementations, ranging from packaged products (commercial off-the-shelf [COTS]) to products purely outsourced or those outsourced via an application service provider (ASP), a custom developed solution, or even a business intelligence data mart or warehousing track. Within routes, there are many phases to choose from. The most common phases and processes, and specifically the ones I've decided to use at the World Wildlife Fund (WWF) include:

1.   A business case justification

2.   A process to gain budgetary approval to fund a requirements analysis or possibly a full project if estimates can be obtained

3.   A detailed requirements analysis

4.   Options for developing a request for information (RFI) or a request for proposal (RFP) for vendors to potentially submit bids for the work

5.   An analysis of available vendors and solutions yielding a vendor/product recommendation

6.   A complete technical architecture analysis, plan, and detailed three-year cost projection, followed by

7.   An implementation process that includes subphases and tasks for system design, development, configuration, data conversion, testing, training, and documentation.

I also recommend including a post-project lessons-learned analysis to document what worked well and what didn't that can potentially help prevent similar mistakes in future projects. The individual phases in a specific route may vary based on the implementation type (see Exhibit 2.3) and can also vary the length of a project. Take for example a custom development route.

While the custom route appears to have fewer steps than others (see Exhibit 2.3), the time for implementation, especially for system design and software development, can be quite lengthy and consume many business and IT resources. The time spent on several other activities, including testing and training, can also vary, depending on the size of a project, the number of technical interfaces in and out of the system, and the number of users that will be supported.

Within each phase in a particular methodology route, there are usually specific sections and templates to be completed that will contain the key details that should be represented by that particular document and deliverable. For example, the business case justification document and template (see Exhibit 2.4) is used at WWF to provide justification, benefits, and proposed

EXHIBIT 2.3   WORLD WILDLIFE FUND METHODOLOGY ROUTES AND MAJOR PHASES (BY IMPLEMENTATION TYPE)

Packaged (COTS)	Outsourced	Custom Developed (Internal)
Business case	Business case	Business case
Budget submission and approval	Budget submission and approval	Budget submission and approval
Form project team, draft project plan	Form project team, draft project plan	Form project team, draft project plan
Requirements analysis	Requirements analysis	Requirements analysis
Develop RFI/RFP	Develop RFI/RFP	Implementation—includes design, development, configuration, data conversion, testing, training, and documentation
Product/vendor analysis, recommendation, and selection	Product/vendor analysis, recommendation, and selection	Postproject lessons learned
Contract negotiations	Contract negotiations	
Technical architecture and total cost recommendation	Implementation—includes design, configuration, data conversion, testing, training, and documentation	
Implementation—includes design, configuration, data conversion, testing, training, and documentation	Postproject lessons learned	
Postproject lessons learned		

RFI, request for information; RFP, request for proposal.

EXHIBIT 2.4   METHODOLOGY PHASE
                   MAJOR SECTIONS

Business Case Justification	Requirements Analysis	Vendor/Product Recommendation
1. Introduction and project objectives	1. Introduction and project overview	1. Introduction
2. List business benefits and metrics for measuring success	2. Current situation and background	2. Requirement rating method overview
3. Funds available	3. Constraints	3. Functional requirements met by product matrix with rating indicators (by mandatory and optional)—section rating at least 60% of overall weight of requirements
4. Resources needed	4. Requirements details (mandatory and optional) that are tied to a key business objective—include functional, technical, security, administration, reporting, interface, and key processing requirements	4. Technical, reporting, administration requirements matrix with rating indicators
5. Timing		5. Vendor analysis profile (creditworthiness, references, product strengths, market share, etc.)
6. Signatures	5. Signatures	6. Total weighted average/score
		7. Signatures

metrics to measure a project's success. The signed business case document is used as a mechanism to help justify investments and is scrutinized during the budgeting process before the organization decides to fund the initiative or whether to simply conduct a more detailed requirements analysis first. The requirements analysis document is the most important document in any systems methodology and is required for all business unit–sponsored projects at WWF. Key components include a current situation analysis, a list of constraints (including funding, staff, expertise, and time), along with detailed functional and technical requirements, usually broken down into one of two categories—mandatory and desirable. Once the requirements analysis is completed and signed by the appropriate signatories, organizations typically have a number of options going forward that include developing an RFP, generating an RFI to gauge interested vendors, or simply proceeding with researching and finding vendor products and solutions that may be suited to meet the detailed needs specified in the requirements analysis document. At WWF, we conduct a comprehensive review of any COTS solution and perform a weighted rating analysis to determine which vendor's product is best suited for our needs and what workarounds we'll need to think about for key requirements that are not met by the vendor's COTS solution.

Buy versus Build

There are several options on the market to purchase a methodology and then potentially customize it to fit a particular organization's needs. Most commercial methodologies today come with applications and predefined templates that are designed to ease the burden of implementation and help IT professionals select the appropriate routes, phases, tasks, and deliverables. But make no mistake—implementing a purchased methodology is not a trivial task and definitely not one to be taken lightly. Most organizations that purchase a methodology build a project team just to determine the routes, phases, and deliverable tasks and then customize the necessary templates for their use out of the many options that are provided by a commercial tool. There are a number of vendors and tools on the market, some with broad and comprehensive offerings. According to a 2002 Forrester Research report, organizations selecting a methodology for packaged software (COTS) should choose wisely and they indicated that: "The strongest methodologies for packaged software implementation have either come from (1) the vendors themselves, usually delivered via training and implementation services, or (2) large or regional systems integrators (SIs)," who have the best experience implementing and using them.[3] According to PricewaterhouseCoopers, their Ascendant methodology, which is available for purchase, contains eight *themes*, including project management, change management, benefits realization, end user education, technical infrastructure, business process, system development, and enterprise risk management.[4]

Most software vendors that produce *packaged* products are increasingly configuring their offerings to reduce the amount of customization by customers and instead building in configurable features to change the functionality of the application to meet their customer's need. Oracle is leading the configure, not customize, mantra, though there are not enough fully implemented references to determine how successful this is, or how configurable Oracle 11i actually is. As an ex-software developer, take it from me—no commercial application will ever fulfill all of a customer's needs without the need for customization or application extension. That said, the real challenge for CIOs and IT professionals is to manage customizations made through sound IT change management practices. More to come on this later in the chapter.

CIOs today have several options when it comes to using methodologies. They can purchase a methodology from a leading vendor and use it *as is* or simply adopt a subset of the processes and templates. Organizations can also develop their own methodology internally or they can leverage consulting engagements and the vendors that provide implementation services to them and adopt their own version as part of a consulting firm–led engagement. Most companies do both. For organizations that are heavy into software development, engineering, or manufacturing, there are additional options to consider, ranging from the Capability Maturity Model Integration (CMMI) to Six Sigma.

Six Sigma

Six Sigma, developed by Motorola in the late 1980s as a method to improve quality in manufacturing processes, is being adopted by some resourceful CIOs. The term *sigma* "refers to standard deviations from an ideal level of operation; put simply, each level of sigma allows for fewer defects than the preceding level," yielding only 3.4 defects per million outputs at level five.[5] At most organizations today, Six Sigma simply means a "measure of quality that strives for near perfection."[6] The main objective of the Six Sigma methodology is to greatly improve the process and design of a product via a very disciplined process improvement strategy with a focus on quality management, improvement, and measurement. There are two core sub-methodologies associated within the Six Sigma methodology: DMAIC (define, measure, analyze, improve, control) and DMADV (define, measure, analyze, design, verify). DMAIC is essentially used to improve upon *existing processes*, whereas DMADV is most commonly used to develop *new products* or processes.[7] Exhibit 2.5 highlights the differences between DMAIC and DMADV.

The typical Six Sigma–led project involves a variety of trained experts to successfully implement quality and process improvement. Green belts (GB) and black belts (BB) are the human implementation arm of the Six Sigma

EXHIBIT 2.5	SIX SIGMA DMAIC AND DMADV SUBMETHODOLOGIES

DMAIC	DMADV
Define the project goals and deliverables	*Define* the project goals and deliverables
Measure the process current performance	*Measure* the needs and specifications
Analyze and determine the root causes for defects	*Analyze* the options to meet needs and specifications
Improve the process and reduce number of defects	*Design* the process to meet customer needs and specifications
Control future process and improve performance	*Verify* the design performance

framework. GBs are essentially employees that have had some Six Sigma training and use the methodology to complete projects. GBs are usually coached by BB, which are the "heart and soul of the Six Sigma initiative" and usually work full-time leading quality projects.[8] A typical BB can complete four to six projects per year, often averaging over $200,000 in savings per project.[9] Process owners (POs) manage the day-to-day processes and employees over a specific business entity and also work with master black belts (MBBs), Six Sigma gurus that oversee a specific business area or function and their employees to achieve exceptional results with quality improvements. At the high end of the Six Sigma organizational chart is the quality leader (QL), who is ultimately responsible for process and quality improvements and is empowered by senior management up to the CEO to help drive defects out of processes and products. General Electric, which started using Six Sigma in 1995, is estimated to have saved $10 billion during the first five years of implementation.[10] In 2003, Mark A. Brewer, senior vice president and CIO of computer manufacturer Seagate Technology, summed up his rationale for using Six Sigma and saving $4.5 million over a two-year period:

> Six Sigma is about taking our IT organization and getting it under control. If I view IT operations as a factory, it's just data centers, networks, servers, VPN, help desks, and so on.[11]

The Capability Maturity Model Integration Frameworks

The CMMI frameworks for process improvement were developed by the Software Engineering Institute (SEI), a federally funded research and development center sponsored by the U.S. Department of Defense, which is operated by Carnegie Mellon University. There are essentially four CMMI models:

1. Systems engineering
2. Software engineering
3. Integrated product and process development (IPPD)
4. Supplier sourcing[12]

The systems engineering module is typically used for the development of total systems, which may include, but is not limited to, software. The commonly used software framework is typically focused on the design, development, implementation, and maintenance of software programs. IPPD uses a systematic approach for product development to ensure that customer needs, expectations, and requirements are met and is usually applied toward another CMMI framework or discipline such as system engineering or software engineering. Supplier sourcing looks to optimize the process involved in complex supplier-to-production solutions.

Within the CMMI model, there are two representations that an organization can choose from: *staged* and *continuous*.[13] The staged option predefines the process areas required to obtain the maturity level rating (1 through 5), provides a single assessment rating that can be compared with other organizations, and is recognized as a best practice approach. In the continuous option, areas are "organized into four process categories: process management, project management, engineering, and support," where maturity levels range from 0 to 5 for each process area.[14] The CMMI model for software engineering (CMMI-SW, v1.1) categorizes the maturity of the software process into five levels, with level 1 being the lowest and least mature and level 5 being the highest rating.[15] Within the framework, maturity levels are defined as incremental accomplishments of process improvement. The higher the maturity level an organization achieves, the higher the probability that an organization can predict future performance at a higher level.

According to Pankaj Jalote, author of *CMM in Practice*, only 20 organizations worldwide have been assessed at level 5.[16] According to the SEI,

CMMI-SW version 1.1, level 1, *initial*, means that essentially no processes have been developed and that processes in support of producing products and services are ad hoc and chaotic.[17] Level 2 indicates a *managed* maturity level with clear processes for requirements management and project planning/monitoring, where the status of projects is visible to management at defined stages and milestones.[18] Level 3, *defined*, indicates that an organization has achieved all the specific goals and processes associated with level 2 and level 3. Level 3 essentially ensures that "all processes are well characterized and understood, and are described in standards, procedures, tools, and methods."[19] The core difference between level 2 and level 3 is that the standards, procedures, tools, and methods are established at an enterprise level and tailored as needed for individual projects. In addition, the details and documentation associated with level 3 are usually much greater and in depth than what is produced in and associated with level 2. Most organizations today strive to meet level 3. Level 4, *quantitatively managed*, focuses on sound organizational process performance and quantitative project management. The primary difference between level 4 and level 3 is that within level 4, "performance of processes is controlled using statistical and other quantitative techniques, and is quantitatively predictable."[20] Most organizations also establish a repository for quality and performance measures to help improve decision making in the future. Level 5, *optimizing*, focuses on innovation and development at an organizational level as well as causal analysis and resolution. At level 5, "processes are concerned with addressing common causes of process variation and changing the process to improve performance (while maintaining statistical performance)."[21]

Since the release of the CMMI product suite in January 2002, many organizations have adopted the methodology and benefited from its use. Simply put, the CMMI framework and models enable organizations to improve processes and develop products and systems with higher degrees of accuracy using a proven and industry-recognized methodology. That said, with any well-defined and structured methodology or framework, there are significant costs and time associated with using and implementing them, specifically in the areas of training and early adoption. Organizations today need to select the right methodology—whether it be CMMI, Six Sigma, vendor developed, or custom built (or a combination of these)—to consistently improve processes, reduce defects, and improve efficiencies.

How important is the use of methodologies in support of system implementations today?

- 66 percent responded with *high.*
- 25 percent responded with *medium.* The remaining responses were categorized as *low* or not applicable.

The CIO of the American Association of Retired Persons (AARP), who was recently recognized in 2003 as one of *CIO* magazine's CIO 100 for IT governance summed up his experience with methodologies:

Unless you have a cadre of trained and certified PMs, buying a methodology and following it loosely can accelerate your ability to take advantage of the benefits of using a methodology.

—John R. Sullivan, CIO, AARP

Another leading CIO adds:

I use a combination. I have to know when and where is best to apply a given methodology, and if it is not available from a vendor in a manner consistent with either the content or approach I require, I develop it internally. The key is not so much sourcing the methodology internally or from a third party, but when and how to choose the right methodology.

—Mykolas Rambus, CIO, W.P. Carey,
CIO *magazine CIO Executive Council Member*

When asked about the primary benefits of using a methodology, the CIO survey group reported the highest votes for the following top three benefits:

1. Enforces discipline, a common approach and consistency
2. Provides for repeatable processes via a framework instead of an ad hoc environment
3. Lowers project risk of failure

Regardless of the specific methodology an IT organization adopts, there can be clear benefits to using one—some quality related, others quantified by hard dollar savings. Thus, professionals desiring to become CIOs should gain some experience with methodologies before they go knocking on an executive recruiter's door and asking for an interview.

PROJECT MANAGEMENT—THE KEY
TO SUCCESS

Project management is an extremely valuable tool and a *must have* skill for professionals wishing to become the CIO or CTO. There are a number of excellent references and books on the market that go into the details associated with forming project teams, developing an effective project plan with full resource utilization, leading teams effectively as a project manager (PM), and mastering the tools on the market to lead a successful project. That said, the purpose of this section is to highlight the need for project management skills, and discuss how CIOs are using project management tools and techniques combined with IT methodologies and organizational structures to deliver solid and repeatable results.

Project plans used as a process and tool for managing the methodology framework phases for a particular route map are very helpful for making a project successful if used effectively. The selection of the PM is one of the most important decisions that can either make or break a project. Detailed project plans take the large, multiple phases associated with a methodology and break them up into smaller, more manageable pieces. Project tasks and dependencies are typically developed in the detailed plan, and resources are assigned to complete specific tasks. Successful organizations have used the project planning process and methodology framework together with a *project organizational structure* to build effective teams. According to a recent *CIO* magazine article in 2004, Mellon Financial has adopted an approach that assigns two PMs, one from IT and the other from the business unit, to serve as co-PMs.[22] In that article, Mellon Financial CIO Alan Wood summed up the benefits: "The dual-manager approach is making the company's project management more predictable and repeatable, with less dependence on individual heroism."[23] At WWF, our capital IT projects that are focused on a business unit(s) solution require multiple co-executive sponsors, including IT, to help build a cohesive team and stress accountability. In addition, we've developed a *project framework and organizational structure* that places accountability in the business unit by assigning the PM role to an individual from the business unit itself or from an external consulting partner that is agreed upon by the business unit (see Exhibit 2.6). From time to time and depending on the project type, we have also implemented co-PMs like Mellon Financial has done. Within our project organizational

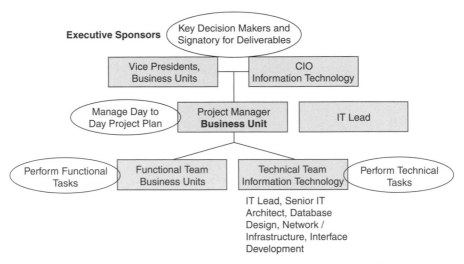

EXHIBIT 2.6   **Project Framework and Organizational Structure**

structure, an IT lead is assigned to each project to assist the PM with project planning as necessary and to provide leadership over all technology-related tasks. WWF IT provides a common set of tools to manage the project as well as mentoring services and project templates in support of our methodology framework to our business unit PMs in order to get them proficient quickly.

I asked a group of CIOs what they thought about the need and importance of project management skills for CIO candidates today.

CIO SURVEY

How important are project management skills and experience for 'first-time' CIO candidates today?

- 80 percent responded with *high.*
- 20 percent responded with *medium.*

Additional comments and advice from our CIO experts is summed up as follows:

Highly important. Successful execution of IT initiatives is a minimally expected quality in CIOs. The ability to successfully deliver results and value in a cost-effective and time-effective manner separates the strategic CIOs from those destined to remain in the back office. The requirement has been laid out by Boards and CEOs of successful companies, as they come to realize the risks of poor IT execution, and at the same time lost opportunity from failed initiatives.

—Mykolas Rambus, CIO, W.P. Carey

If you are not a good PM, you should not be a CIO. That said, PMs should be delegated. CIOs at all levels should be masters of account-ability management, not just project management, since projects typ-ically make up less than 30 percent of what the total function really does each year.

—John Von Stein, Executive Vice President and CIO,
The Options Clearing Corporation

Project management skills are very important—but from an experi-ence level. I don't believe CIOs should be leading projects. CIOs should be on project executive steering committees.

—Carol F. Knouse. SVP and CIO, The Donna Karan Company LLC,
eWeek Corporate Partner and Advisory Board Member

IT CHANGE MANAGEMENT—THE KEY TO MINIMIZING UNNECESSARY DOWNTIME

IT change management is what I refer to as the *third leg* in the triple crown of IT best practices associated with systems implementation and service management. A classic definition for IT change management might look something like this: *Change management includes all tasks associated with man-aging the design, development, testing, and implementation of technical changes to a production system environment. Included are operational procedures, manage-ment processes, and transaction-based systems in support of scheduling, approving, and coordinating system changes.* In reality, I would simplify the definition as: *proactively managing technical infrastructure and application changes to minimize risk to production systems and increase system availability.* A recent Forrester Research report indicates that the analyst "believes that infrastructure change management—because it puts IT firmly in control of the infrastructure—is the necessary first step in the BSM [business service management] direc-tion."[24] Due to today's predominantly decentralized and commodity-based computing environments, change can occur at a variety of levels within an

Typical Production System Hierarchy

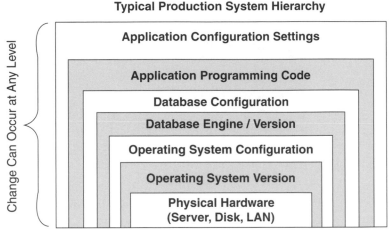

EXHIBIT 2.7   IT Change Matrix—Today's Systems Are Complex

organization (see Exhibit 2.7). In most cases, a change to a production system usually results in multiple changes at a variety of levels, from physical hardware to an application configuration change or upgrade.

Regardless of the layer, IT professionals must test the appropriate change before putting it into production. The major steps usually associated with infrastructure and application change management include the following:

- Identify the need for a change request (CR).
- Categorize the CR and submit it as a change candidate, possibly to the change control board (CCB). Some examples include hardware device upgrade or repair, software patch, application upgrade, data fix/change, configuration change, etc.
- Determine the impact of the change.
- Approve the CR and assign it to a resource.
- Document steps to perform the change, and develop a test and roll-back plan.
- Conduct testing (may include IT and business unit involvement).
- Submit the CR for approval to move to production.
- Approve the CR for production migration.
- Notify users of any anticipated downtime (if any).

- Implement the CR in production and log any outages. Roll back the change if necessary according to documented roll-back procedures.

- Document any results or lessons learned from the change implementation.

- Close the CR.

Organizations that have large complex environments often make use of a change control board or CCB to help coordinate and approve changes to large production systems. Depending on the type of change, there may be different processes, tasks, and approvals throughout the process. Take, for example, a business unit application upgrade or patch. The processes, workflow testing, and approvals can differ depending on the type of change request (see Exhibit 2.8). Also, depending on who is actually applying the change, processes must be clearly defined. At WWF, some of our internal enterprise resource planning (ERP) system changes are actually made with support directly from our vendor or by a business system owner. As a result, our change management processes and systems at WWF have to be flexible enough to include third-party vendors as well as internal IT and business unit staff.

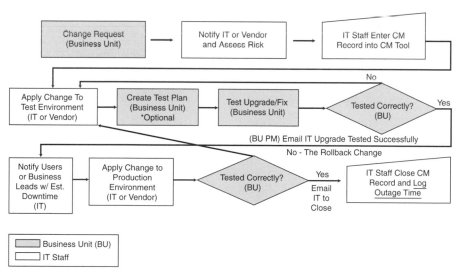

EXHIBIT 2.8   Change Management Framework—Business Unit Application Upgrade or Patch

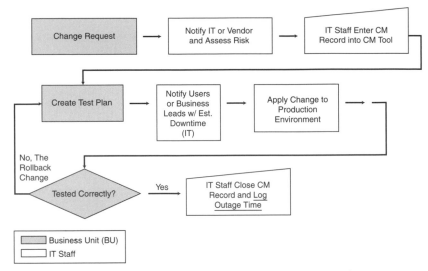

EXHIBIT 2.9   **Change Management Framework—
IT Hardware Upgrade** (Example: Server, Disk, or
Memory Upgrade)

A simple hardware change, however, most likely will not require involvement from business unit staff, so the change request process would involve a different workflow (see Exhibit 2.9).

CHANGE MANAGEMENT AUTOMATION TOOLS

There are three real approaches to infrastructure and application change management today:

1. Making changes in an ad hoc fashion without any centralized management or documentation

2. Managing change via a procedural and manual process with documentation

3. Using an automated tool and database to enter, track, and report on changes.

For obvious reasons, the first option is not recommended, but I am still surprised by the number of organizations that don't use a defined process or system to apply changes to production system environments. Smaller organizations or ones that are strapped for cash usually implement manual processes and checkpoints. Small to large organizations, however, are encouraged to look at utilizing an automated solution, which can either be a custom-developed solution or one purchased from a vendor. If purchased, there are a number of mature tools and commercial products on the market to help automate and ease the burden of managing the many technical changes that occur in most organizations today. The best commercial tools also support processes and best practices that are defined by the industry-recognized Information Technology Infrastructure Library (ITIL), which was introduced by the Office of the Government of Commerce (OGC) in 1989.[25] Automated tools from vendors like BMC Remedy, Peregrine, Tripwire, and Telelogic provide solutions that offer effective control and reporting to manage the changes associated with today's computing environment, including network management, database management systems, ERP systems, security management, and storage systems. Automated tools can also provide effective workflow engines to help automate the change request process as typical change request ownership and approval moves from person to person. Some of the key benefits of an automated solution are reporting ease and having a central repository for storing and querying past changes, serving as a mild knowledge repository. With increasingly more investigative IT audits and the enactment of legislation like the Sarbanes-Oxley Act of 2002, reporting and compliance is playing an ever more important role in information technology. Today, nonprofit organizations don't have to comply with section 404 (internal controls and procedures) of the Sarbanes-Oxley Act. However, auditors are increasingly conducting technical audits with more stringent procedures and requests for information. Today, it's common for an auditor to ask for a report of *all system changes*, by date and type, made to any mission-critical production systems that either track revenue or store financial data.

Organizations that outsource or use ASP vendors must ensure that those vendors also use best practices for applying changes to production systems. Thus, simply outsourcing a system without proper due diligence will not guarantee system operability and reliability to an organization's end user base. Change management is an internal and external process that needs to be directed by CIOs and carefully managed by IT professionals, consultants, vendors, and partners. Failure to pay attention to the change process at any layer, physical to application, can only result in less stable systems and angry users.

WHAT DID I DO TO PREPARE?

After completing my graduate degree in business with a concentration on technology management, I went to work for PriceWaterhouse LLP as a principal consultant, specifically to gain experience with methodologies and large system implementations. During my time at Price, I worked with customers in support of large ERP system implementations, web-based reporting solutions, and business intelligence systems. In the late 1990s, I took my first step into the nonprofit arena and accepted a position with AARP as the head of software development, e-business, database management systems, and business intelligence. During my time at AARP, I worked with other seasoned IT professionals in selecting and implementing a commercial methodology to be used in the organization. In 2001, I was appointed the vice president and CIO of WWF. Shortly after joining WWF and assessing the needs of the organization, we implemented a customized methodology and change management system along with a set of processes in support of system implementations and production system service management. Today, those methods, processes, and procedures are used on all projects that have a business unit sponsor or are associated with large IT capital initiatives, and have resulted in repeated successful project implementations by helping to nail down requirements, mitigate scope creep, and deliver systems that add value to the organization.

RECOMMENDATIONS

While methodologies, IT change management, and project management are not especially sexy topics, they do serve a valid purpose in world-class organizations today and help to deliver repeatable successes in support of the business. The following recommendations are designed to help candidates gain the skills needed to serve in an IT leadership role:

- If you are not using methodologies in your current organization, start by conducting research on the top firms that provide them for sale and engage your CIO in a discussion with other key staff on their benefits and whether there may be an opportunity to use them in your firm.

- I highly recommend getting some consulting experience with an organization that uses methodologies effectively in consulting engagements at some time in your career. There is no better experience than learning and applying methodologies in support of medium to large scale consulting engagements and system implementations.

- If you are involved in software development or anticipate having oversight of a software development department, you should get up to speed with the processes and levels associated with the Capability Maturity Model Integration (CMMI) for software development. CMMI is a great framework for improving the quality of software development initiatives.

- Get up to speed on IT change management processes and tools. CIOs today that are using change management effectively in their organizations experience less unscheduled system downtime and are more proactive than reactive by not having to constantly put out fires associated with poorly planned changes to production systems that cause problems. In addition, as a CIO, you'll likely have to produce detailed reports in support of the annual IT audit, depicting all changes made to any financial and revenue systems.

- Attend vendor demos and seminars for products and services associated with methodologies, project management, and change management systems and tools.

- Take a course in project management and get some experience serving as a PM or an IT lead for a business unit application or system implementation. For those who want to gain superior project management skills, enroll in a certification program and become certified as a Project Management Professional (PMP) with the Project Management Institute. While not needed for a CIO role, the experience and knowledge can be invaluable.

ENDNOTES

1. Peter Drucker, www.quotationspage.com (accessed March 27, 2005).
2. David B. Guralnik, Editor in Chief, *Webster's New World Dictionary of the American Language*, Second College Edition (Springfield, MA: William Collins and the World Publishing Company, 1978), 894.

3. Liz Barnett, "Methodologies for Package Software—Don't Choose in a Vacuum," (June 17, 2002) (Cambridge, MA: Forrester Research), www.forrester.com/Research/Print/LegacyIT/0,7208,27135,00.html (accessed March 28, 2005).

4. "Our Methodology," PricewaterhouseCoopers web site, www.pwc.com/extweb/service.nsf/docid//D90812B7B0B9504985256D16003BCD9C (accessed March 28, 2005).

5. Edward Prewitt, "Six Sigma Comes to IT," *CIO* magazine, www.cio.com/archive/081503/sigma.html (accessed March 28, 2005).

6. Charles Waxer, "Six Sigma—What Is Six Sigma?" iSixSigma LLC, www.isixsigma.com/sixsigma/six_sigma.asp (accessed April 6, 2005).

7. Ibid.

8. Charles Waxer, "Six Sigma Organizational Architecture," iSixSigma LLC, www.isixsigma.com/sixsigma/six_sigma.asp (accessed April 6, 2005).

9. Ibid.

10. Waxer, "Six Sigma—What Is Six Sigma?"

11. Steve Ulfelder, "The Power of Two. Mellon Financial Is Implementing an IT-Business Team Approach to Managing Its Most Complicated Projects," *CIO* magazine (September 15, 2004), www.cio.com/archive/091504/mellon.html (accessed March 28, 2005).

12. Software Engineering Institute's web site, www.sei.cmu.edu/cmmi/adoption/cmmi-discs.html (accessed April 6, 2005).

13. Software Engineering Institute's web site, www.sei.cmu.edu/news-at-sei/features/2003/4q03/feature-1-4q03.html (accessed April 6, 2005).

14. Ibid.

15. Software Engineering Institute's web site, www.sei.cmu.edu/cmm (accessed March 28, 2005).

16. Pankaj Jalote, *CMM in Practice. Processes for Executing Software Projects at Infosys* (Boston: Addison-Wesley, October 22, 1999), 1.

17. CMM Product Team, Technical Report CMU-SEI-2002-TR-029, CMMI for Software Engineering, Version 1.1 Staged Representation (CMMI-SW, V1.1 Staged), www.sei.cmu.edu/publications/documents/02.reports/02tr029.html (accessed April 29, 2005).

18. Ibid.

19. Ibid.

20. Ibid.

21. Ibid.

22. Ulfelder, "The Power of Two. Mellon Financial Is Implementing an IT-Business Team Approach to Managing Its Most Complicated Projects."

23. Ibid.

24. Jean-Pierre Barbani, "Infrastructure Change Management Is the Key to Business Service Management," Quick Take, Forrester Research (September 10, 2004), www.forrester.com/Research/Print/Document/0,7211,35352,00.html (accessed March 29, 2005).

25. Peregrine Systems web site, www.peregrine.com/products/ITIL.asp (accessed March 29, 2005).

CHAPTER 3

IT Standards and Governance

The difference between a boss and a leader: a boss says "Go!"—a leader says "Let's go!"

—E.M. KELLY[1]

THE IMPORTANCE AND BENEFITS OF IT GOVERNANCE

IT Governance Defined

Webster's dictionary defines governance as "the act, manner, function, or power of government."[2] To extrapolate from the word *govern*, Webster's continues with the definition: "to exercise authority over; rule, administer, direct, control, manage, etc."[3] Today, IT governance is a hot topic and one that deserves a lot of attention from both professionals aspiring to become CIOs and existing IT executives. I have a theory that most CIOs who didn't have an IT governance structure and plan before the IT bubble in 2001 got one quickly as their budgets got slashed and they were forced to deliver more with less. In general, the CIO is responsible for managing the information technology and investments for an organization to ensure that they effectively align the use of technology with the goals of the organization. Forrest Research defines IT governance at the most basic definition as "the process of making decisions about IT."[4] The article goes on to list the four main objectives of IT governance as *IT value and alignment, risk management, accountability,* and *performance measurement.*[5] A recent *CIO* magazine article on IT governance frameworks stressed that there is no one-size-fits-all structure, but that successful IT governance models

> strongly embed an enterprise's culture, processes, and values. While there are guidelines, there are no "one-size-fits-all" frameworks. IT executives should evaluate many areas, including business alignment, fiscal controls, development methods and standards, management accountability, organization structure, outsourcing options, procurement standards, and quality initiatives, as elements of an approach to IT governance.[6]

The IT Governance Institute defines IT governance as "the responsibility of the board of directors and executive management. It is an integral part of enterprise governance and consists of the leadership and organisational structures and processes that ensure that the organisation's IT sustains and extends the organisation's strategies and objectives."[7] Peter Weill and Jeanne Ross, two industry leading experts on IT governance and authors of *IT Governance: How Top Performers Manage IT Decision Rights for Superior Results*, provide the best definition I've seen: "the decision rights and accountability framework for encouraging desirable behavior in the use of IT."[8] Weill and Ross go on to describe that the framework includes the following five key areas and decisions:

1. IT principles
2. IT architecture decisions and directions
3. IT infrastructure for shared IT services
4. Business application requirements for each project
5. IT investment and prioritization[9]

Forrester Research adds to their definition that a good IT governance framework is based on three elements:

*   Structure—who makes the decisions and what organizational structures are part of the plan?
*   Process—how are IT investments made and what processes aid the approval and prioritization for investments?

- Communication—what are the methods of communication to stakeholders such as the board of director, senior management, IT staff, employees, and other stakeholders such as third-party vendors?[10]

IT Governance Purpose and Benefits

Organizations that adopt a best practice IT governance model and structure will yield some clear benefits and avoid several risks associated with business application and IT-related projects. Specifically, IT governance is intended to provide the following benefits to organizations:

- Better align IT with business goals and units
- Deliver technical solutions that meet business objectives
- Control costs associated with infrastructure and projects
- Manage and monitor the joint IT-business unit portfolio of projects
- Maximize IT and business unit resources
- Comply with audit, regulatory, and legal mandates
- Manage IT-related risk

Risk always surrounds the information technology community of professionals. The *always on* computing environment of today demands that organizations around the globe use technology in almost every facet of their business. That said, the costs associated with IT-related failures, whether infrastructure outage related or overruns for project costs for large enterprise resource planning (ERP) solutions, are real and expensive. Organizations that fail to employ an appropriate IT governance structure simply put themselves at risk and will likely spend more on IT-related expenditures as part of their normal operating environment. Top performing organizations with solid IT governance structures typically perform better and save money. According to a *CIO* magazine article by Peter Weill and Jeanne Ross, "Companies with better than average IT governance can earn at least a 20 percent higher return on assets than organizations with weak governance."[11] Weill and Ross go on to emphasize that "top performing companies rely on a set of governance techniques that are simple, reinforcing, coherent and explainable, and that engage key decision-makers."[12] Simply put, IT governance benefits organizations by enabling them to be more successful by linking technology with business objectives via measured goals, without excessive spending.

In 2002, I rolled out an IT governance framework at the World Wildlife Fund (WWF) intended to align IT with the rest of the organization and deliver clear and perceived value from our business unit customers and donors at the best possible price. At its core, the WWF IT governance framework has the following components: (1) IT principles, policies, and procedures; (2) IT architecture, hardware, and software standards; (3) project methodologies and templates; (4) project management office and project plan templates that maximize organizational resources and stress business unit ownership; (5) IT change management; (6) audit, regulatory, and legal compliance; and (7) IT strategies, investments, and budgeting (see Exhibit 3.1).

The governance model at WWF, which includes a project methodology and framework, IT change management, and IT standards, is at the center of how the IT team develops and delivers complex solutions and support services to our customers in support of the WWF conservation mission. In addition to the core IT governance *domains*, the IT strategy is designed to integrate with the rest of the organization via a number of externally focused connectors. Specifically, these touch points include involving the management committee, business customers and owners, project managers,

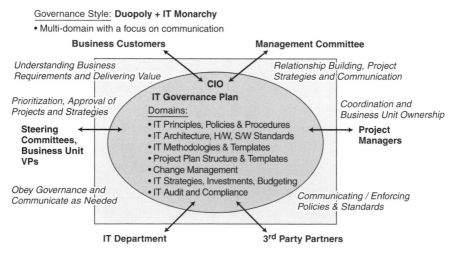

EXHIBIT 3.1   IT Governance at World Wildlife Fund
H/W, hardware; S/W, software.

third-party vendors, IT staff, and a variety of steering committees appropriately represented by business unit vice presidents (VPs), process experts, and other key decision makers. The model has brought together diverse teams of professionals and helped to create effective teams working toward common goals and objectives using repeatable processes and clearly stated IT principles, policies, and procedures. I asked my distinguished CIO survey group how they valued IT standards and governance in their organization.

CIO SURVEY

How important are IT standards and governance models to you as a CIO?

- 75 percent responded with *high*
- 16.5 percent responded with *medium*
- The remaining responses were categorized as *low* or not applicable

Forrester Research recently got together a group of 135 IT decision-makers to discuss what works well with regards to running a well tuned IT governance process. The respondents that participated indicated that IT governance was important and provided the following additional information:

- The primary reasons for formalizing an IT governance plan are to better align IT with the business strategy (83 percent), improve the value from IT (70 percent), improve risk management and compliance (67 percent), improve operational performance (62 percent), and reduce IT costs (45 percent).

- CIOs are the main IT governance leaders (55 percent), followed by CIO designates (18 percent).

- 55 percent of respondents reported that they have an IT governance framework in place, 29 percent indicated that they were working to establish one, but 17 percent indicated that they have no plans for establishing a governance plan.

- The primary driver for IT governance has been the IT organization (54 percent), followed by corporate governance (39 percent).

- IT governance is mainly a custom effort. Even with published frameworks like COBIT and ITIL, 54 percent of respondents indicated that they had developed their IT governance framework in-house. Consultant custom-developed frameworks accounted for 23 percent, followed by 20 percent for COBIT and 19 percent for ITIL.[13]

Additional techniques often used by CIOs to help build the right governance model include:

- Separate core IT infrastructure from discretionary IT investments and budget for core support infrastructure separately from IT investments that directly involve or benefit business units. Engage business leads in discretionary system spending and establish business ownership where appropriate to help fund and champion those systems and enhancements.

- Focus on the process and desired outcomes instead of a specific vendor-driven solution for business unit applications. Use methodologies where appropriate to drive requirements that are owned by the business unit.

- Educate other executives about the IT governance plan and raise awareness for why policies and procedures are put in place and the benefits that they can yield.

IT Governance Types and Structures

There are several different governance types, and, depending on the source, they can range from being described in simplistic terms and conditions to full complex strategies, methods, and diagrams. Forrester Research breaks down IT governance structures into four types: *centralized, decentralized, federated,* and *project based.*[14] The typical IT centralized model is exactly that—centralized and managed in IT, where most if not all of the decisions regarding IT investment and budgeting take place. The real risk in a centralized model is that information technology departments and most notably the CIO may inadvertently block input from other business units, resulting in decisions being made in a vacuum without real consideration from others, especially those tightly tied to revenue and product growth. In contrast, a purely decentralized structure is often a chaotic approach to technology management, since each decentralized IT function can have its own governance process in different business units, including IT standards, processes, and decision-making, resulting in a lost opportunity for gaining purchasing economies of scale for technology infrastructure, support, and services. Organizations that typically adopt a purely decentralized model are usually trying to make faster decisions or implement system solutions more quickly and think that cutting out IT can get the job done in less time. In doing so, they must either establish mini-IT disciplines, usually not tied to the broader IT organizational function, or rely on external consultants for solutions. Either way, a decentralized model that doesn't involve the IT team, tools, and processes used in a best practice IT governance plan adds risk and usually increases operating costs. In many instances, organizations that use a decentralized governance structure cannot truly garnish the benefits associated with a solid IT governance environment. They often end up with duplicate infrastructures, applications, and technical support functions and share little if any knowledge with other business units, resulting in stove piped systems that don't focus on enterprise goals and don't take advantage of enterprise economies of scale opportunities to reduce costs while delivering results. A federated structure contains components from both a centralized and decentralized model. Most often in this model, IT infrastructure and enterprise applications are run from a centralized perspective and owner, while business units retain control over their applications, development resources, and system enhancements. The federal model has been used frequently in government, including federal, state, and local sectors. The federal model is often difficult to implement, since organization leaders at the enterprise level often have different concerns from the various business unit leaders. In this model, the business units with the largest budgets usually have the most influence on the decision-making process. Thus, the challenge for the federated model is to respond to the individual needs of various business units, while still attempting to conform to enterprise-wide IT architecture standards and platforms. The project-based structure is derived from the consulting industry and is a combination of both central and decentralized structures with a twist. In this model, most of the IT resources are centralized and report to the office of the CIO, but application development resources are pooled and grouped together as organizational structures themselves in support of specific project teams as centers of competency. The challenge for organizations that adopt a project-based structure is to ensure that there are strong governance processes for project selection, prioritization, and funding.

Jeanne Ross and Peter Weill categorize IT governance structures as *archetypes* of one of the following types: business monarchy, IT monarchy, feudal, federal, IT duopoly, and anarchy.[15] In a *business monarchy*, essentially all decisions are made within the business unit with little or no input from the IT team. The *IT monarchy* is the inverse of the business monarchy and risks pushing key business unit and technical decisions into the office of the CIO, possibly alienating the business units themselves. The *feudal* model is usually made up of several business unit leaders and process owners. Ross and Weill indicated in their study of 256 organizations that the *feudal* model was the least common approach used in IT governance today.[16] The type that I was drawn to the most in the *CIO* magazine article by Weill and Ross was that of an *IT duopoly* option. A duopoly strategy essentially shares key decision making for IT budgets, applications, and technologies between IT and one business unit, with participation usually at the CXO, business unit VP, or process leader/group level. An *anarchy* approach essentially means that all decisions and processes are ad hoc and not structured, which can produce varied results at best and not scale across the enterprise to meet organizational goals.

Ross and Weill go on to discuss how their framework (IT principles, IT architecture decisions and directions, IT infrastructure for shared IT services, business application requirements, and IT investments), when applied properly to various input and decision makers in an organization, can yield better results and higher performance.[17] This is what differentiates their IT governance model from others. I strongly believe that no single governance structure works for all organizations. That said, the right combination of archetypes paired with a core framework may lead to a best practice approach and model. According to Jeanne and Peter and after researching governance structures in 256 organizations, they found that the top three performing organizations reported having the following input/decision matrix across their framework[18] (see Exhibit 3.2).

The research by Weill and Ross showed that the top three IT governance performers exhibited a combination of archetypes, most commonly IT duopoly, IT monarchy, and business monarchy to make decisions. Regardless of the IT governance structure/framework selected, other

	IT Principles	IT Architecture	IT Infrastructure Strategies	Business Application Needs	IT Investment
Business Monarchy	3	3	3		2 3
IT Monarchy		1 2	1 2	1	
Feudal					
Federal				1 3	
IT Duopoly	1 2			2	1

EXHIBIT 3.2   **Top Performing Governance Decision Matrix**

Source: Adapted from Peter Weill and Jeanne Ross, *IT Governance,* Cambridge, MA: Harvard Business School Press.

senior managers from the business side of the organization should be involved in major IT decisions and strategies, especially ones that affect them or their business unit and performance. At WWF, the executive committee, the leadership team, other business unit VPs, the chief of staff, the CFO, and sometimes the CEO have input into decisions that affect the IT budget, project approval, and prioritization. That said, the IT governance plan in place at WWF is one that is flexible enough to ask for input where necessary yet make the appropriate *monarchy* and *duopoly* decisions where necessary (see Exhibit 3.3). According to the *CIO* magazine article by Ross and Weill, "top governance performers had more direct involvement by senior management than non-top performers. The more involvement, the better the governance performance."[19]

IT governance and decision making at WWF uses predominantly a *federal* archetype for input into IT principles, IT architecture, IT infrastructure strategies, and investments. However, most of the decisions are made in IT, thus utilizing an IT monarchy. The obvious exception that is clearly highlighted in Exhibit 3.3 is for business applications. IT most often pairs with a business unit for input and requirements in solving a particular business need where a clear system owner can be established. For those types of systems and solutions, WWF typically utilizes an IT duopoly strategy. In

	IT Principles Input / Decision		IT Architecture Input / Decision		IT Infrastructure Strategies Input / Decision		Business App. Needs Input / Decision		IT Investment Input / Decision	
Business Monarchy										X
IT Monarchy		X		X		X					
Feudal											
Federal	X		X		X				X	
IT Duopoly							X	X		

EXHIBIT 3.3   IT Governance Decision Making at World Wildlife Fund

Source: Adapted from Peter Weill and Jeanne Ross, *IT Governance,* Cambridge, MA: Harvard Business School Press.

situations where there are multiple business units associated with a strategy or goal, we often expand this strategy to include multiple business owners and plug-in IT where necessary. That said, the key component is to involve the business units in the application-driven solutions and facilitate ways for them to take direct ownership, but work as a team to accomplish the stated goals.

When I asked a group of world-class CIOs about their governance structure and approach, the answers varied widely from organization to organization, which indicated to me that in many organizations, the right approach and model is still evolving.

CIO SURVEY

What IT governance styles or models do you use and why?
- The majority of CIOs responding indicated that they used *multiple* governance styles in their organization, most notably a combination of *federal, IT duopoly,* and *IT monarchy.*
- There was a tie for second place, where respondents indicated the same number of votes for only one type of structure used— *federal or duopoly.*
- The next most common answer was for a *business monarchy or IT monarchy.*

- Interestingly, 20 percent of respondents indicated that they had no formal IT governance process at all.

In addition to defined governance structures and types, several organizational committees usually are formed to keep the governance process from becoming a stale framework. According to a recent *CIO* magazine article on IT governance hierarchy at State Street, the financial firm employs several committees and groups, each with a different focus to define strategy, make decisions, and then execute. State Street utilizes an *operating group*, made up of the CEO, CIO, vice chairman, CFO, head of human resources, and three business unit executive vice presidents (EVPs) to meet weekly to create business strategy.[20] In addition, they have an *executive steering group*, with membership similar to the operating group less the chairman and two EVPs that meet once or twice a month to discuss IT and operations issues and make decisions on projects costing up to $10 million.[21] State Street also maintains an *IT council* to discuss IT best practices, an *office of strategy and governance*, made up of IT and select business divisions, along with an *integration project management office* that meets twice per month to discuss day-to-day integration details associated with a recent bank acquisition.[22] In short, State Street and many other organizations have clearly defined committees and teams to support their IT governance model and stay focused on a constantly changing business environment and set of organizational needs. The level and number of committees and their membership will clearly vary from one organization to another, depending on a variety of factors, such as size, culture, time, and willingness to participate. As Exhibit 3.1 indicates, WWF's governance hierarchy provides support for a number of committees and steering groups to help make the right decisions on budgets, project prioritization, technology standards, and principles with appropriate communication between business units, IT staff, and third-party vendors to ensure that goals are met and IT is properly aligned with the needs of the business.

Governance Frameworks

There are a number of frameworks available that can be researched to find helpful models for establishing an IT governance plan. CobiT, ITIL, and

ISO17799 are great places to start. CobiT, developed by the Information Systems Audit and Control Association (ISACA), is fast becoming an industry-accepted standard for materials related to IT governance. To date, the CobiT framework is strong in controls and metrics, and breaks down IT into a set of processes across multiple domains: *planning and organization, acquisition and implementation, delivery and support,* and *monitoring,* with each process containing a number of high-level control objectives.[23] The CobiT framework essentially helps IT professionals by giving advice on what to do. The IT Infrastructure Library (ITIL), initially developed in the United Kingdom by the Office of Government and Commerce (OGC), consists of several guides ranging from service support, to delivery, security management, application management, and infrastructure management.[24] The ITIL documents are more *process* oriented and focus on identifying IT best practice services. The International Organization for Standardization (ISO), which developed ISO 17799, titled "Information Technology—Code of Practice for Information Security Management," was released in December 2000 and focuses on IT security planning.[25] While it serves as a thorough resource in itself, the core focus of ISO 17799 is on security and thus is applicable to only a portion of the typical IT governance plan. Other areas of reference for IT governance structures, plans, and best practices include IT advisory research firms, published works from reputable authors, articles from reputable information technology magazines, and conversations with peers from other organizations. I've found peer discussions to be most helpful in learning what other organizations have done and what works best within their culture. I can't stress enough the importance of peer networking in the role of becoming a CIO and operating effectively as one. I have found discussions with other CIOs in organizations around the world to be one of the most useful tools in establishing best practices to date. Thus, don't reinvent the wheel when looking to gather information on IT governance models and best practices. There is plenty of information available to get started with developing an effective IT governance plan, and networking with peers should be at the center of that fact finding before deciding on a final structure.

IT POLICIES AND PROCEDURES

At WWF, IT policies and procedures are designed to give guidance to our end users and business unit staff on topics that include a technology usage policy and many other specific policies and procedures that surround a plethora of technologies like e-mail, instant messaging, Internet access, wireless technologies, and the like (see Exhibit 3.4). Thus, policies at WWF support the IT principles and speak to the *what* type of questions from users. Additional key policies (as noted in Exhibit 3.4) include data backup and retention, purchasing, and the specifics surrounding network and application accounts and passwords that include naming conventions, password complexity requirements, grace logins, and account activation/ termination. Procedures, however, were developed to speak to the *how*, such as how to request access to a mission-critical application or a specific role/module within one, or how to apply for an asset (personal computer [PC], server, laptop, etc.) that is being decommissioned at WWF U.S. headquarters, but may have value and a limited useful life at another WWF family office around the globe, where funds may be an issue in keeping up with the latest technology.

Procedures should serve as the *how to* guide for staff to accomplish something that is related to or impacted by technology. In addition to standard procedures such as technology purchasing, desktop/laptop refresh, system/

EXHIBIT 3.4   IT POLICIES AND PROCEDURES

Policies	Procedures
Technology usage	Inventory and asset control
Asset redistribution and	Purchasing
disposal	Telecommuting
Data backup (PCs/servers)	IT advisory services
Network accounts	IT satellite office assessments
E-mail	Asset redistribution and disposal
Account naming conventions	Disaster recovery
File attachment blocking	SPAM portal management
Accounts (consultants, temps)	Virus detection and notification
Space quotas	Deploying software across the network
Purging/archiving	Third-party software installs
SPAM	Access to ERP/mission-critical applications
Instant messaging	Online meetings
Purchasing	Project methodology and templates
Internet access	
Laptops as PCs	
Wireless technologies	

application access requests, advisory research requests, steps to request an IT supported personal digital assistant [PDA], and the use of mobile satellite terminals and phones, WWF procedures include information on how to use the project methodology and templates along with the procedures associated with IT change management and the steps that include requesting a change, approving a request, testing, approval, and migrating application and infrastructure changes into production.

IT STANDARDS

Hardware Standards, Software Standards, and Architecture Standards

IT standards are also a big part of the IT governance plan in most organizations and usually the easiest to define and enforce. IT standards should be applied across a wide range of technologies:

- Telecommunications infrastructure, protocols, and products
- Desktop and laptop PC hardware vendors and models
- Server vendors/models
- Desktop and server operating systems, and database management system software
- Application software
- Application development tools
- Messaging systems and platforms
- Wireless technologies (including PDAs)
- Security solutions and products
- Middleware systems and application servers
- Business intelligence software
- Reporting products
- Desktop productivity suites/offerings

Organizations that employ IT standards usually benefit in a variety of ways, most notably:

- Saving time and meeting customer and business user needs more quickly.

- Reducing the cost of products and services by leveraging economies of scale, buying in larger quantities, and reducing the number of service level agreements (SLAs) to draft and negotiate.

- Reducing staff, vendor support costs, and infrastructure costs by supporting fewer products and systems.

- Focusing on the right staff skill sets for a limited number of products and services that meet business objectives.

- Increasing flexibility in the enterprise by building a scalable and reliable technical infrastructure that can be easily integrated where necessary to improve the flow of information across systems.

At WWF, input for IT standards does come from the business units via a *federal* approach for general technology and via an *IT duopoly* for business application or integration requests, resulting in infrastructure decisions made via a combination of IT and one or more business units. Simply put, the more technology options (hardware and software) used in an organization, the more expensive it usually is to purchase and support the various solutions and integration between related systems. Organizations that use IT standards correctly can achieve greater system uptime percentages, maximize resources and skill sets to support them, and leverage economies of scale for purchasing. A lack of IT standards can dramatically increase costs and create support problems, especially if there are no decisions on which technology to adopt. The financial impacts of IT standardization are not usually realized when a new technology or product is launched, but once expertise and support is mature and purchased quantities of a product or solution reach levels that support reductions in cost and ownership via economies of scale (see Exhibit 3.5). IT professionals that ignore standards or adopt fragmented approaches towards IT standardization will see their costs continue to rise beyond the ramp-up period of those technologies and will find it difficult to support a full heterogeneous infrastructure that can quickly get out of control (see Exhibit 3.6).

The Key Benefits of Database Standardization

According to a Forrester Research article on database technology standards, organizations "should standardize on one or two key enterprise DBMSes to improve manageability, enhance service level agreements, and

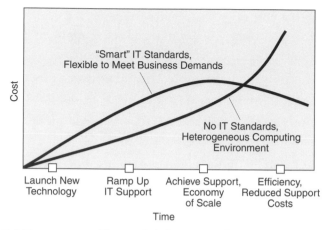

EXHIBIT 3.5   Financial Impact of IT Standards

save money."[26] Many organizations that lack IT governance frameworks usually have lax IT standards on hardware and software. Database software systems today are complex and require a unique skill set to properly support them. Organizations that maintain many different products such as IBM DB2, Microsoft SQLServer, Oracle, Postgress, MySQL, Ingress, Informix, and Sybase on a variety of hardware platforms and operating systems such as MVS, AIX, Solaris, HP-UX, Windows, and Linux add significant complexity for IT organizations to properly manage their database environment, plan for upgrades, integrate heterogeneous products, and manage security. Thus, the key benefits to database standardization include:

- Reduce staff costs and skills required
- Reduce licensing costs by leveraging economies of scale surrounding less products supported and more licenses of those that are
- Easier database administration and support
- Simplified database disaster recovery
- Decreased cost and complexity for data security
- Increased optimization of database integration via fewer interfaces to support between vendor products

When standardizing on database products, IT staff are encouraged to look at the business drivers and needs of the organization (and their applications)

EXHIBIT 3.6   IT STANDARD TYPES

Software	Hardware
PC/laptop operating system	Business class PDAs
Antivirus	PC vendor/models
Anti-SPAM	Satellite phones/terminals
Instant messaging	Networking equipment (switches, routers)
Software distribution	Security appliances
Patch management	Server vendor/models
Remote access	
Office productivity suite	
Web collaboration	
Internet browser	
Server operating systems	
ERP	
Database management	
Business intelligence	
Software development tools	
Application server software	

first, since many application products on the market today support only a limited number of database vendors. Once isolated, IT staff must determine the features needed, the skill sets required to support, and the threshold for tolerance on entry price and maintenance, which can vary widely between offerings. Finally, staff must take into consideration a database vendor's market share and operating install base. Simply put, application developers and commercial offerings write their applications to the largest percentage of the database market first, and consider alternative offerings with a lower percentage of market share second. IT advisory research firms are a great way to research database vendor install bases and market share percentages.

According to a Forrester Research article on technology and product standards, "technical architecture and standards do not just happen" by themselves.[27] It takes planning and communication with the right business units to establish standards that work for an organization and don't appear to constrict or prohibit growth in the right areas. Forrester Research recommends that IT organizations tighten the IT governance process, implement technical standards and architectures, and adopt product standards in order to truly save time, reduce internal and vendor costs, and add flexibility for growth and scalability.[28]

Total Cost of Ownership

Total cost of ownership (TCO) is a term that has been used, misused, and misconstrued over the past decade or so when it comes to tracking the actual cost of ownership for a particular type of technology, most often hardware. As an example, I've read many articles that attempt to find the actual cost to purchase, install (hardware and software), maintain, and provide technical support and training for a typical desktop computer in a business or corporate environment. Depending on the number of years in service, usually two to four, the typical PC can cost an organization anywhere from $5,000 to $10,000 when all costs, hard and soft, are included. I'll be honest—it is difficult to identify the actual cost of an IT component or application, but you can get close enough to help shape IT strategies and standards to optimize computing environments and look for cost reductions. Thus, don't get too involved in TCO numbers, but use it as an approach to analyze purchasing and standardizing on the right hardware and software. For example, does it cost an organization more or less to support multiple desktop vendors and multiple PC productivity software suites? The answer is yes—so you should make an effort to standardize on the right product for your organization from hardware to software. The TCO approach can be helpful when determining the proper IT standards for the following technologies. When combined with looking at business and technical requirements and risk factors, TCO has helped me determine the right mix for several technologies, including (1) fiber versus SCSI versus SATA for storage area networks; (2) rack-mounted xU servers versus blades; (3) physical technical support staff versus virtual via remote management tools, standards, and policies; and (4) maximizing processor and storage capacity in servers. The bottom line is not to get too caught up in TCO as a sole technique for identifying the actual costs, but using it to help look for ways to reduce costs and increase operating efficiencies. At WWF, I challenge my technical staff to analyze existing technologies, standards, and solutions and come up with recommendations to improve them while reducing costs and still providing best practice levels of service. TCO combined with IT standards for hardware and software can get you there if you don't get too bogged down in the numbers. I asked the distinguished CIO group their thoughts on the importance and benefits of IT standards across different technology offerings. Their results were predictable and in line with my expectations.

What are the top five benefits of implementing IT standards for hardware, software, databases, and architectures?

- The top answer, with 80 percent of the vote, was to *reduce financial costs of running IT.*
- The second highest response was that IT standards *reduce maintenance needs.*
- The third highest response was that standards optimize IT skill sets applied to less technology and, thus, create more efficiency.
- The fourth highest response was that standards maximize purchasing power and leverage with vendors.
- The last of the top five responses was that IT standards minimize the complexity of the IT architecture and blueprint.

Project Portfolio Management—Use It or Lose It

Project portfolio management of IT-related projects in an organization today is critical and almost a necessity to properly plan for, evaluate, prioritize, monitor/manage, and track projects. The typical decision to start a project management office or capacity is often made as a result of things slipping through the cracks, causing multiple project overruns, increases in cost, or projects that are implemented that don't actually properly align with the business needs of an organization. Just how many organizations are using project portfolio management (PPM) today? It's tough to tell. A Forrester Research report indicated that the market for PPM is on the verge of a boom, partially as a result of recent vendor consolidations in the marketplace.[29] According to a recent report by AMR Research, "As many as 75 percent of IT organizations have little oversight over their project portfolios and employ non–repeatable, chaotic planning approaches."[30]

For organizations or IT professionals not using project portfolio management that are having problems with project evaluation, approval, and implementation, PPM can likely help gain control over their IT organizations and add a valuable component to an IT governance model. Simply put, organizations that have enough projects in the pipeline, are trying to manage IT investments tied to business goals and objectives, and are not consistently meeting expectations of their customers, should consider project portfolio management. A well-running project portfolio management process, when combined with other elements of the IT governance plan, such as methodologies and IT standards, can provide the following benefits:

- Maximize IT investments while minimizing risk

- Improve communication between IT professionals and business and process leaders, thus opening the door to better IT alignment and more frequent communication with business leads

- Allow staff to better plan for resource allocation and identify areas where resource and skill constraints may affect a project before it's too late

- Reduce the number of redundant projects

- Make it easier to stop a project that is not properly aligned or performing well[31]

Regardless of the approach or software used, there is no one-size-fits-all solution when it comes to project portfolio management. There are, however, plenty of resources and guidelines for implementing a best practice PPM and project management office. A recent *CIO* magazine article provided the following key steps to establishing and managing IT projects:

- Perform an inventory of IT and business unit–related projects.

- Set up a process to evaluate candidate projects to ensure that they fit with a strategic objective.

- Create a fair process that includes business unit involvement to prioritize approved projects.

- Actively manage and review project status.[32]

In 2005, WWF established a project portfolio management component to the IT governance plan. It is used in conjunction with our IT project methodology, which essentially means that business unit project candidate requests must go through some fleshing out, preferably via a business unit justification, before being considered as *real* project candidates considered for funding. In addition, all funded major projects that come into the IT project portfolio must go through a formal requirements analysis before a solution is defined. The key components to the WWF project management office (see Exhibit 3.7) include processes and software for (1) identifying and tracking the IT project portfolio at any state in the life of a project, (2) ensuring proper communication to identify business unit project candidates and review proposed business cases and metrics for measuring success, (3) using the IT balanced scorecard to determine IT infrastructure project candidates, (4) approving projects, (5) prioritizing projects, (6) implementing projects, (7) monitoring project status (both detail and overall health), (8) and measuring overall results and lessons learned. The most valuable component and payoff of the WWF portfolio approach is in the evaluation of project candidates and prioritization. Projects that are submitted for consideration that don't meet a clear business objective or strategy are not usually recommended or approved for funding, saving the organization time and money, and ensuring that only projects that are properly aligned with strategic goals of the organization get approved. Without a formal process, the likelihood that rogue projects slip through and get implemented is much greater. The project prioritization function at WWF also helps WWF better manage resources and other constraints that often arise with a full pipeline of project candidates. Simply put, most organizations have more requests than they can actually deliver in a given fiscal year. Project prioritization, when used and discussed with key business unit partners, is an excellent way to create a *shared portfolio approach* where project ownership is established and communication is open to discuss projects, resource management, and other measurable constraints.

Tools

There are a variety of tools on the market, from desktop software such as Microsoft Excel and Projects, to expensive commercial offerings that can help IT professionals manage their projects and portfolios today. Keep in mind, a software solution will not solve all of your PPM issues with a simple purchase order. The concept sounds actually quite simple, but in reality

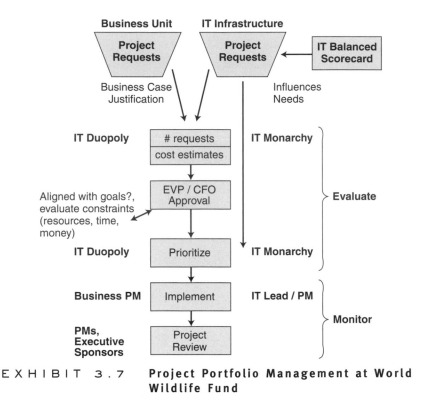

EXHIBIT   3.7   **Project Portfolio Management at World Wildlife Fund**

PPM takes time, resources, and effective software solutions to properly manage a portfolio of technical projects that involve both IT-only infrastructure and business unit–related application system initiatives. WWF uses several tools in support of project portfolio management, most notably Microsoft Projects 2003 Server for detailed project plans and a custom system to monitor and manage the project portfolio and individual project health ratings. According to a *CIO* magazine article, "In 2002, the portfolio management tool market was about $85 million; and could exceed $540 million by 2005."[33] A Forrester Research article that surveyed CIOs found that the majority of organizations that utilized portfolio management software were using off-the-shelf spreadsheet tools, followed by a minority using either a commercially developed product or home-grown application.[34] Organizations that use a custom-built solution may look toward inexpensive tools like Microsoft Access or Excel to build solutions that don't require the full set of features, or the cost, usually associated with a commercial offering. For commercial offerings, complexity of requirements often determines the product selected, but there are plenty to evaluate on the market. I recommend developing internal requirements for a PPM system before making a decision and use IT advisory services and peer networking to find out what works best for others before deciding to write the check. Simply put, purchasing a commercial PPM tool is the easiest part of the implementation. I asked several of my colleagues what they used for project portfolio management, and their answers were consistent with recent IT advisory research.

CIO SURVEY

Do you use a third-party software product to manage projects as a portfolio? If so, which one?

- 40 percent responded that they use a commercial third-party solution for enterprise project portfolio management.
- 25 percent responded that they used a combination of Microsoft Projects and a custom-built solution.
- 25 percent responded that they used just Microsoft Projects to manage their portfolio.
- 10 percent responded that they did not use a software solution to manage their portfolio of projects.

IT STRATEGIES, INVESTMENTS, AND BUDGETING

IT investments are tied to IT and organization strategies and should be managed with care. It is paramount that CIOs today understand the business needs of an organization and map a short- and long-range strategy to meet those needs. At WWF, our strategies are broken down into two separate approaches: *IT infrastructure* and *business goals/objectives*. WWF budgets for infrastructure and defines strategies to ensure appropriate technology refresh and application upgrades in support of core technology to run the business independently with justification from that for business unit–sponsored projects. In addition, we partner with our business units, learn their needs, apply methodologies to collect and analyze requirements, and then define short- and longer-range strategies to develop, acquire, and/or outsource appropriate application technology to meet those specific business goals and objectives. That said, midlevel and senior IT staff today must understand the business drivers and goals to properly develop tactical and strategic plans for delivery. The operational aspect of IT is easier. If you get the wrong strategy, you'll spend a lot of money on the wrong technologies.

Developing an IT strategic plan is time consuming, but rewarding if done properly. According to a 2002 Forrester Research report, "Good plans explicitly link IT projects to the direction of the business."[35] Forrester goes on to say that the attributes of good IT strategic plans

- are persuasive and communicated to other senior managers.
- use objective methods for evaluating IT investments.
- consider constraints, including costs and resources.
- exploit the planning process and use it to educate business unit leads.
- define structures and processes to maintain the plan.[36]

There are many resources to help IT professionals create and manage their IT strategic plan. The purpose of this text and chapter is not to detail the components of an IT strategic plan, but to emphasize that they are necessary and part of the IT governance plan. Before developing a strategic plan and laying out the budget to justify IT investment, it is important that CIOs and IT professionals with budget and signatory authority understand the business goals and strategies for the organization first—more on this in the next chapter. In addition, IT investments and budgeting are covered in more detail in the second half of the book.

COMMUNICATING IT STANDARDS, POLICIES, AND PROCESSES

Much of the governance framework at WWF focuses on a multidirection communications strategy that is designed to keep the IT team engaged with our business customers, keep our management committee informed,

CIO SURVEY QUESTION

How do you communicate IT standards, governance policies, and procedures outside of the IT group? The top five answers are as follows:

- The top answer, with 60 percent of the vote, was via written IT policy statements, most often posted on the corporate IT intranet.
- The second highest response was by communication with the management committee, either verbally or in written reports.
- The third most common response was via e-mail communication to staff.
- The fourth highest response was via briefings and demonstrations to staff.
- The fifth highest response was via publications in human resources training manuals that initiated in the office of the CIO.

keep our project managers (IT and business) focused on executing projects via the developed methodology framework, and ensure that our third-party vendors comply with our governance structure and standards and execute best practices (see Exhibit 3.1). Communicating IT governance to the rest of the organization is of paramount importance. CIO Peter Weill, in his study of 250 organizations, said that "the higher the percentage of managers who could describe governance, the higher the governance performance." [37] Education is key to demystifying IT and the methods to ensure proper technology use and alignment.

Regardless of how and where IT governance plans, policies, standards, procedures, and portfolio management are communicated to staff, it probably isn't enough. An IT governance plan and structure is large, complex, and made of many processes and procedures. It's not just how you communicate a governance plan, it's how often.

WHAT DID I DO TO PREPARE?

Not enough and I was lucky. Shortly after taking the CIO helm as the CIO of WWF, the terrorist attack of September 11 struck the United States, and most nonprofit organizations saw a greatly diminished fund-raising environment that decreased revenue and lasted almost two years. Budgets were cut across the board and I had to quickly come up to speed on IT governance and best practices to deliver more with less. The result of our hard work, which involved many folks, including the EVP, operations, IT staff, and the CFO, yielded a leaner IT organization with solid governance framework that enabled our organization to deliver results with less money. In 2003, WWF was recognized by *CIO* magazine as one of the top 100 *most resourceful* organizations at the 16ᵗʰ annual CIO 100 awards ceremony in Colorado Spring, Colorado. We won the award for our efforts surrounding IT governance.

RECOMMENDATIONS

To close this chapter out, I advise professionals aspiring to become CIOs to not lose focus on the core technology skills that are necessary to run a world-class IT shop. Individuals today are more in charge of their career than ever before. Planning your career earlier, while setting clear, measured, and obtainable goals can get you to where you want to be if you are persistent and patient. The following recommendations are designed to help candidates prepare for an IT leadership role:

- Read *IT Governance*, by Peter Weill and Jeanne Ross. It's an excellent book that takes a very research-oriented approach to reviewing how some of the best companies in the world manage their IT investments and systems.

- Initiate discussions with your supervisor and CIO to learn more about the governance process in your organization. Research IT advisory notes and publications in reputable IT trade magazines for best practices approaches to IT governance. Don't re-invent the wheel. Make formal recommendations where appropriate to improve your governance structure once you've done your homework. Keep focused on controlling or reducing costs, delivering value and projects that are aligned with the business and creating effective and not overburdening standards in support of strategic goals.

- Research vendor solutions for the right project portfolio management tool that fits your organizations needs and budget. Don't just purchase a tier-1 product with the hopes that it will solve all your portfolio management problems.

- Evaluate vendor options and technologies to help drive effective IT standards in your organization that are pertinent in your area of the IT organization. This will lay the framework for a consistent approach that can be applied to other IT disciplines that make up the office of the CIO when you land your first position.

- Stay focused on improving your communication skills and look for opportunities to communicate to staff where appropriate orally and in writing. CIOs must have excellent communication skills and strategies and are constantly challenged to find ways to break down IT speak into business terms.

- Network with peers and find out what works well in their environment with regard to IT governance and project portfolio management. Leverage best practices of other organizations and make recommendations where appropriate to improve your plan and structure.

ENDNOTES

1. E.M. Kelly, www.quotationspage.com (accessed March 29, 2005).

2. David B. Guralnik, Editor in Chief, *Webster's New World Dictionary of the American Language*, Second College Edition (Springfield, MA: William Collins and the World Publishing Company, 1978), 605.

3. Guralnik, Editor in Chief, Webster's New World Dictionary of the American Language, 604.

4. Craig Symons, Marc Cecere, G. Oliver Young, Natalie Lambert, "IT Governance Framework" (Cambridge, MA: Forrester Research), March 29, 2005, www.forrester.com/Research/Print/Document/0,7211,36563,00.html (accessed March 30, 2005).

5. Ibid.

6. Ron Exler, "IT Governance Frameworks," Analysts Corner, *CIO* magazine (July 10, 2003), www2.cio.com/analyst/report1559.html (accessed March 29, 2005).

7. "Board Briefing on IT Governance," 2nd ed., English version, IT Governance Institute, online research web site, www.itgi.org/template_ITGI.cfm?Section= About_IT_Governance1&Template=/ContentManagement/HTMLDisplay.cfm &ContentID=19119 (accessed April 29, 2005).

8. Jeanne Ross and Peter Weill, "Recipe for Good Governance," *CIO* magazine, 36 (June 15, 2004), 36–42.

9. Ibid.

10. Symons et al., "IT Governance Framework."

11. Jeanne Ross and Peter Weill, "Recipe for Good Governance," *CIO* magazine, 36, (June 15, 2004): 36-42.

12. Ibid.

13. Craig Symons, "IT Governance Survey Results," (Cambridge, MA: Forrester Research), April 14, 2005.

14. Symons et al., "IT Governance Framework."

15. Ross and Weill, "Recipe for Good Governance."

16. Ibid.

17. Ibid.

18. Ibid.

19. Ibid.

20. Author unknown, "A Higher Power," Sidebar: State Street's Governance Hierarchy, *CIO* magazine, 36 (March 15, 2004), www.cio.com/archive/031505/state_sidebar_one.html (accessed April 29, 2005).

21. Ibid.

22. Ibid.

23. Craig Symons, Adam Brown, "IT Governance and the Balanced Scorecard" (Cambridge, MA: Forrester Research), August 20, 2004, www.forrester.com/Research/Print/Document/0,7211,35233,00.html (accessed March 30, 2005).

24. Ibid.

25. Ibid.

26. Noel Yuhanna, Mike Gilpin, Kimberly Q. Dowling, "Standardize on Enterprise DBMSes" (Cambridge, MA: Forrester Research), June 25, 2004.

27. Chip Gliedman, "Making Technologies and Products Standard" (Cambridge, MA: Forrester Research), March 11, 2005, www.forrester.com/Research/Print/Document/0,7211,36513,00.html (accessed March 14, 2005).

28. Ibid.

29. Margo Visitacion with Carl Zetie, "PPM Market in Transition" (Cambridge, MA: Forrester Research), December 10, 2004.

30. Todd Datz, "Portfolio Management—How to Do it Right," *CIO* magazine, May 1, 2003, www.cio.com/archive/050103/portfolio.html (accessed March 27, 2005).

31. Ibid.

32. Ibid.

33. Ibid.

34. Visitacion et al., "Portfolio Management Tools."

35. Marc Cecere, "Planning Assumption" (Cambridge, MA: Forrester Research), February 13, 2003, www.forrester.com/Research/Print/LegacyIT/0,7208,29350,00.html (accessed April 18, 2005).

36. Ibid.

CHAPTER 4

Learn the Business and Build Key Relationships

Individual commitment to a group effort—that is what makes a team work, a company work, a society work, a civilization work.

—VINCE LOMBARDI[1]

THINK LIKE A CONSULTANT TO LEARN THE BUSINESS

Getting IT staffers to think like the business is a challenge.

Many technology professionals merely look to the capabilities of a product or solution, hardware or software, to maintain and grow the IT infrastructure. Success in the field of information technology today is way beyond just maintaining the data center. It involves integrating IT staffers at all levels with the business units to *understand* their needs before attempting to *solve* them. CIOs today that embrace this approach are getting better results than ever. According to a *TechRepublic* article, "the CIO's first priority is to understand the business."[2] The *TechRepublic* article goes on to suggest that effective CIOs are able to

- assess business needs quickly.
- identify technology issues and risks.

- define IT plans, strategies, and initiatives to meet business needs.

- assist with prioritizing initiatives.

- build an IT organization and focus on good IT governance.

- manage the IT budget cost effectively.

- use technology to drive positive change to improve profitability, productivity, and other important company objectives.[3]

CIOs who have a broad base of experience and who focus on learning the business also have more portability when it comes to moving from one organization to the next or changing sectors. Successful CIOs and IT underlings who adopt a simple approach to learning the business and understanding the drivers for improvement will be more successful than those who simply focus on the technology component associated with the role of the CIO. That said, I've been successful in the past by taking a consultancy approach to learning the business in a variety of firms. Effective consultants use a variety of tools and skills to flesh out business requirements, identify pain points, prioritize issues, and map a strategy to deliver results. Some of the best experience I've ever gotten was serving as a consultant in both a regional U.S. company and at a worldwide big-four consulting firm. Effective consultants usually have the following qualities:

- They have good listening skills and are patient with their customers.

- They have a broad range of experience that spans across multiple business sectors and industries.

- They are analytical.

- They have excellent verbal and written communication skills.

- They have access to other resources and information knowledge repositories to assist with developing best practice solutions that add value.

- They utilize a methodology or a series of repeatable processes to gather requirements, develop process improvement, follow change management best-practices, and have an implementation strategy to achieve consistent results.

Getting IT staffers to think like a consultant can sometimes be difficult, but it is not an impossible feat. Effective CIOs often utilize the tools and processes found in good IT governance plans to get their staff to *think like consultants*. At the World Wildlife Fund (WWF), the IT governance plan is central to our strategy of treating our internal business customers, external donors, and third-party vendors in a manner that can produce repeatable and consistent results. Specifically, methodologies, templates, project planning tools, and change management practices are effective tools in helping to build cohesive technical and business project teams to flesh out requirements and develop solutions that deliver results. Other ways to help drive a consultancy approach within an IT department include

- hiring external consultants and process experts to drive projects and internal teams.

- training IT and business unit team members via seminars and targeted training classes on project management and methodologies.

- augmenting existing skills by encouraging IT staff to expand their business knowledge by enrolling in outside educational programs such as project management certificate courses, MBA programs, or other educational certificates and curriculum that will build and strengthen effective IT-to-business skills.

- attending industry conferences and seminars that focus on building better business skills and partnerships.

According to a recent *ComputerWeekly.com* article, "IT directors have to expand on their role to become business leaders."[4] Informal networking organizations such as the British Computer Society's elite group, CIO-Connect, provide effective networking forums and conferences that facilitate sharing best practices.[5] According to founder John Handby, former IT head of technology for GlaxoSmithKline and the Royal Mail, "CIO-Connect is specifically designed for the managers who report directly to the CIO."[6] Handby continues, "It offers a series of leadership briefings aimed at those who CIOs typically rely on for news on technology and what they need to learn next."[7] At the pre-CIO level, forums like CIO-Connect focus on strategies and techniques to groom the next generation of IT leaders in areas that include (1) interacting with other senior executives, (2) effective communication skills and techniques, and (3) how to demonstrate IT value. In addition to these types of forums, there are a variety of other fee-for-service seminars that offer training on financial skills, writing proposals, contract and vendor negotiation techniques, methodologies, IT governance, and developing an effective IT strategic plan. *CIO* magazine also just recently launched a conference in 2005 that focuses on the "Ones to Watch," with a number of sessions and discussions on IT leadership that targets the next generation of IT leaders.[8] Regardless of the forum or approach used, IT professionals that desire to rise to the executive technical leadership ranks should start thinking like a consultant and get a broad and diverse set of experiences that focus on learning the business.

HOW TO BUILD EFFECTIVE RELATIONSHIPS—INTERNAL AND EXTERNAL

Building effective relationships with internal business customers and other executives is an essential today for any CIO. Relationships are often built on a combination of respect and trust. That said, CIOs today spend a significant amount of time working with peers in other business units along with key third-party vendors to deliver solutions to problems that can help build that trust and deliver value to the organization. Learning the business via interacting with other company executives is one of the best ways to increase the exposure of the information technology group and establish credible and beneficial relationships. This can be done in a number of ways, which include (1) raising awareness of the IT function to non-IT staff, (2) working with other executives on strategic plans and initiatives to drive the organization forward, (3) demonstrating non-IT strategic and business skills outside of the normal role of the CIO, and (4) serving as a co-executive sponsor on projects with a business unit.

Convincing peers that IT is a valued player in the organization can be easy or hard, and sometimes both in the same organization. John J. Ciulla, former chief information officer at Tivoli Systems, ran a series of internal campaigns to reach out from the IT group to raise awareness[9]:

> Our slogan for the first campaign was "We're All in the Same Boat," and to kick it off, we painted a canoe with Tivoli colors, filled it with ice and beer, and presented it to the rest of the company at a Friday afternoon beer bash.[10]

According to Ciulla, the campaign efforts got folks around the organization to notice the IT department and better understand what they stood for. Ciulla summed that up: "The effort brought us together as a team."[11]

Working with other executives on strategic plans and initiatives also helps raise awareness of the IT function, but more importantly gets CIOs closer to the business side of the house, which in turn will help them better understand the business goals and drivers for success. CIOs that spend time outside of IT projects are often rewarded with other non-IT leadership tasks. Demonstrating strategic skills outside of the CIO role helps build credibility with other executives and can lead to greater involvement in non-IT strategic initiatives. Tivoli's CIO did just that and was rewarded by being appointed to lead their company's leadership and communications task force, where he gained more exposure to the COO and CEO levels.[12] Serving as a co-executive sponsor on a project with a business unit is also a great way to establish a trusted relationship with a business peer and learn the business. Co-executive sponsors help build a team-oriented group from the top down and can accentuate that the *team* is working to accomplish the goals of the project together. It also is a great mechanism to ensure that responsibility and accountability for key projects is shared. Accountability and ownership for projects at the business level usually translate into more time spent planning, evaluating progress, and motivating a team to be successful. As stated earlier in this book, all significant projects at WWF that have a capital impact and investment have multiple co-executive sponsors who share in the work, accountability, and success. The result for me has been a better working relationship with business unit peers and established trust from successful projects.

External relationships with key consulting partners and outsource providers can be as important as developing internal relationships. If your strategy is to rely on external ASP-like solutions, you had better have a good relationship with your vendor, since they can make or break your credibility with your internal customers. In reality, internal business customers and users could care less whether an external vendor that provides critical services to an organization fails or if the internal IT team screws up. Accountability still falls on the CIO as the one who ultimately selects and approves vendors. Thus, to users, vendors are agnostic and IT is still responsible. That said, select your vendors and external partners carefully.

Chapter eight provides some good insights into how to best select and manage an external vendor so that they become a partner and not just an outsource provider. Up-and-comer CIOs should take note of these techniques and start working to build their *business portfolio* of successes and accomplishments. That, combined with solid technical skills and other recommendations and strategies laid out in this book, will help get you closer to a shot at becoming a world-class CIO.

GETTING QUICK WINS TO ESTABLISH CREDIBILITY AND TRUST

CIOs need to be acutely aware of an organization's pain points and develop reliable solutions to resolve them quickly. In addition, CIOs today need to have excellent financial management skills to properly communicate and build effective relationships with other business executives, including the COO and the CEO. According to a *TechRepublic* article, "being able to relate well with the CEO and CFO in financial terms is extremely important. It's not something you can fake." [13] Getting quick wins in early as an IT professional in a new organization or role is extremely important. Technology professionals need to continually work with their customers and business partners to identify the highest-priority issues and get them solved quickly. Driving partnerships on key projects can be a helpful way to tackle the toughest projects and demonstrate results. In addition, technology pilots are a great way to go after issues where you may not have the best solution but are trying to quickly fix a pain point/project and can take some risk to get there quicker.

Once you've established some trust via a few key quick wins, you have a basis to go after the longer-term projects and issues. Thus, today's IT professionals are encouraged to go after the *low hanging fruit* early and then develop a clear strategy and plan for tackling the longer-term problems together with trusted business partners who can help share in the responsibility and assume ownership of solutions and systems to drive successful results.

I asked a group of leading CIOs their thoughts on how important it was to learn the business and why IT professionals and executives can no longer just rely on running the data center to meet expectations. CIOs must deliver results based on what the business needs.

What are the top three benefits of establishing and maintaining relationships with your business customers?

- The top answer was to get buy in for projects and yield better implementation success.
- The second highest response was to develop mutual respect, trust, and credibility.
- The third most common response was to better understand the customer's needs (both present and future) and determine how IT can help service them.

What percentage of your time do you spend focusing on relationships and projects associated with business units outside of IT?

Of the responses that gave a percentage,

- The *average* response was 54 percent.
- The *highest* response was 90 percent.
- The *lowest* response was 15 percent.

What steps do you take to foster *team integration* between IT and business unit staff for joint projects?

I ask customers to become part of the project team. I prefer them to actually drive and lead the project. They identify the business needs and help break down any barriers. They define ROI.

—*Earl Monsour, Director, Strategic Information Technologies,*
Maricopa Community College District

Ensure that users are participating in the decision making process. Ensure that users are participating throughout implementation, configuration, and deployment. There should also be a good signoff process.

—*Shyam K. Dunna, CIO/Assistant General Manager, MARTA*
(Metropolitan Atlanta Rapid Transit Authority)

Except for some internal infrastructure improvements, all projects are joint projects and the first thing we do at the kick-off is have all team members attend a one-half day project management course that we developed in house.

—*Carol F. Knouse, Senior Vice President and CIO, The Donna*
Karan Company LLC

Four ways: (1) Business unit leaders and IT jointly prioritize projects across business areas; (2) business unit and IT co-project manage initiatives; (3) we hold regular status meetings with senior business management, senior IT management, and project management teams working on the business/tech initiative; and (4) we reward team collaboration at the successful conclusion of significant milestones throughout the project.

—Steven W. Agnoli, CIO, Kirkpatrick &
Lockhart Nicholson Graham LLP

At the inception of any project, two teams are created. One team is the executive group that is responsible for the overall project. This includes the key stakeholders from both IT and the business. The other team is the actual project core team, which is responsible for delivering the project. Both of these teams meet on a regular basis to insure the success of the project.

—Hans Keller, CTO, National Aquarium in Baltimore

Our project office includes business representatives and use developed methodologies that require participation, testing, and security.

—Ray Barnard, Vice President and CIO, Fluor Corporation

A formal project management methodology and various informal opportunities for our internal customers and IT to interact. We schedule at least monthly cocktail hours and make it a point to personally invite as many of our internal customers as possible.

—Mykolas Rambus, CIO, W.P. Carey

FOCUS ON DELIVERY, DELIVERY, DELIVERY

Results speak louder than anything else and help build relationships with key members of the staff. CIOs today that don't deliver results will simply not have trust from their customers and risk being out of a job if they can't establish it and build solid relationships. When I first started as the CIO at WWF, I spent a significant amount of time interviewing business unit staff and other executives to find out what was working well and what wasn't from a technology perspective. In my discussions, I took great notes and listened to my peers and their subordinates without offering much advice during the interview process. This was the time for them to talk and me to listen. I documented all the issues and developed a chart of all the pros and cons of how IT was *perceived*. In addition, I noted all the issues and requests for assistance, ranked them appropriately, and validated my list with the business units. The top pain points and issues that spanned across multiple business units were at the top of my list and the issues that had the least financial impact associated with an individual department were listed last. I then developed a plan to tackle the most pressing issues and was able to set up joint IT-business unit projects where we shared in the responsibility and ownership of projects. Within six to nine months, the WWF team and our consulting partners were able to deliver some clear results, which included (1) a new and improved secure remote access solution, (2) a major upgrade to a financial system, (3) improvements in the IT infrastructure that resulted in improved reliability, and (4) a newly deployed customer enterprise resource planning (ERP) system. Those deployments and accomplishments helped build a more cohesive IT/business unit team and better trust with my business unit peers. I then started mapping out the IT strategy and governance plan for WWF that, when completed, helped drive additional successful projects, increase cost savings, and build solid relationships that were based on trust and credibility.

Some organizations are trying new and different approaches to solve business problems. According to a recent *CIO* magazine article:

> [M]ore and more companies are pulling IT staff out of the business unit where they've been assigned, and placing them in specialized business process or skill set groupings, to be called out to serve on project teams whichever needed in the enterprise.[14]

Champions of this model hail the benefits of joint IT-business unit teams, but most IT staffers are used to a home, whether it be in IT or assigned permanently to a business unit. So, CIOs are challenged daily to flex and stretch the traditional IT centralized model to a fully decentralized one that can yield results, but at a cost. According to *CIO* magazine, "the pressure to recentralize as a means to eliminate redundancy is absolute nonsense because for every dollar saved, $2 will be spent (secretly) in uncoordinated, nonstandard, unsupportable IT efforts in the field. And if you go this route, you may as well say goodbye to any chance of your staff's truly understanding the business."[15]

Managing expectations is also a critical part of establishing relationships and trust. Overpromising and underdelivering is a recipe for failure.

According to the *CIO* magazine State of the CIO 2004, "the biggest challenge for CIOs is business executives' unrealistic expectations of what IT can do."[16] The article goes on to suggest ways to overcome this challenge:

- *Get your IT house in order.* Signs of a problematic IT shop include (1) delays in projects, (2) an unclear IT governance structure, (3) a poor IT organizational structure, (4) no IT strategic plan, and (5) a consistent set of missed projects and failed deliveries.

- *Listen.* IT shops can't truly solve business unit problems if they don't understand them. That involves listening carefully to your customers and knowing when to ask the right questions to facilitate more information flow to IT.

- *Educate your customers.* Educate your customers on well-developed methodologies, the IT governance plan, and how it can be used along with project management to get key issues and problems resolved. At the end of the day, processes and procedures can be extremely helpful in determining what the problem is and how to solve it. Signatures on deliverables are another great way to help build accountability and ownership, which, if results follow, can lead to trust.

- *Communicate early and often.* Managing expectations is about effective communication. If you think that an approach is wrong, say so and recommend an alternative strategy. True IT leaders know that it's okay to say no when an approach is wrong. Also, there is no harm in trying to overcommunicate.[17]

I've run the WWF's IT shop like a business from day one. While I recognize and respect the WWF mission and commitment to saving life on Earth, I run IT like a business. Simply put, other than the mission and the tax status, the IT department at WWF is run like a for-profit business with an eye on results and a constant focus on how money is spent. Some organizations take running IT like a business literally. In the late 1990s, USAA's IT spending was growing faster than the business, and they were bleeding money from two major failed IT investments.[18] USAA decided to start running their IT shop like a business. They implemented several measures to help that included (1) using IT charge backs, (2) turning their IT services and technologies into 200+ products with annual flat rates, and

(3) managing the IT operation as a profit and loss (P&L) environment with all profits being reinvested in new technology development.[19] In a recent 2004 article, an IT vice president (VP) at USAA, Joe Thomas, said, "I often joke that I used to be in IT."[20] The article goes on to point out that "the punch line is that he's still in IT—specifically ITCO (Information Technology Co.), the wholly owned IT subsidiary that serves the financial services" giant.[21] Thomas is one of several IT VPs at USAA who report to the president of ITCO, whom most would refer to as the CIO, but whom USAA refers to as the "chief executive, running IT with a profit and loss statement."[22] Thus, whether you're running an IT subsidiary with your own profit and loss (P&L) or a typical IT department with high demands from customers, you have to learn the business in order to deliver results time and time again. In today's high-paced technology-dependent environment, consistency is rewarded with a paycheck. Inconsistent results are rewarded with a pink slip.

WHAT DID I DO TO PREPARE?

I have always forced myself to *think like a consultant and focus on the business*, then develop solutions like an IT professional. Fifty percent of my career has been spent on the consulting side of IT implementations, while the other half was spent managing technology for organizations internally. I've never forgotten my role as a consultant and have actually applied it to internal IT departments. That said, my modus operandi has always been to (1) run my IT department like an internal consultancy and business, (2) force myself to probe and learn the business, (3) always put the organization's goals first, not an individual department's, (4) forge joint teams to solve complex problems and deliver solutions, and (5) do due diligence to determine how to solve problems once well-documented requirements are known and signed off.

RECOMMENDATIONS

This one is easy for me to answer, because my approach has not changed in almost 20 years of increasing IT responsibility:

- In any role, at any level, engage your existing and prospective customers. Listening skills are just as important as any other skill. Those who don't listen will never learn the business. Don't just rely on your assumptions, let the business unit tell you about their issues, priorities, and problems, and then help them take ownership for delivering results. They'll feel a lot better than if IT just rammed a solution down their throats—even if was the right solution.

- In order to develop trust, you must be able to deliver results once key issues are uncovered. Delivering results is the best way to gain an ally going forward, who may help you lobby for resources and budgets in the future.

- Use methodologies and business case templates to help the business units flesh out the real and important requirements. Always get a signature on the scope and detail associated with *what* is to be done. The IT side is the *how*.

- Think like a consultant. On complex issues that may be political in nature, it always helps to think outside of the box—almost as if you were not part of the organization itself. That way, you're almost guaranteed to recommend the right solution and not get tied up with politics and department infighting. If necessary, bring in an external consultant to help flesh out the issues, needs, and requirements from a fresh and neutral perspective. Engage the business unit and let them evaluate and agree upon the right consulting partner before hiring to get additional buy in.

- Always do what is best for the business and not a particular department.

- Reward teams that do a great job and produce results. For successful implementations, make the business unit look good and recognize key accomplishments where appropriate. This helps build that much needed trust and bond between IT and the business units. Where appropriate, submit key accomplishments and projects for outside awards. External recognition of joint team performance is an excellent way to build a well-oiled and focused team.

- Get experience on large projects as the IT lead and facilitate ownership and project management in the actual business unit (or co-ownership with IT as an alternative). Where available, take responsibility of the IT budget and expenses for projects. Experience in managing the financial aspects of a project can be just as important as managing the project tasks and deliverables themselves.

- Get some exposure with key vendors that help IT deliver results and take responsibility for managing vendors and their services. Vendors and their products and solutions are very important in today's IT environment and can make or break a reputation and trust with your business customers. Spend a lot of time negotiating third-party services and don't underestimate service level agreements (SLAs) and key contract terms and conditions. At the end of the day, if your vendor fails and you don't have an alternative, you could fail, too. I don't know of a single IT shop that does it all without key support from vendors and third party partners.

ENDNOTES

1. E.M. Kelly, www.quotationspage.com (accessed March 29, 2005).
2. Michael Sisco, "The CIO's First Priority is to Understand the Business," *TechRepublic* (May 10, 2004), www.techrepublic.com.com/5102-6298-5198191 .html (accessed April 18, 2005).
3. Ibid.
4. Julia Vowler, "How IT Managers Can Learn the Business," *ComputerWeekly.com* (September 23, 2003), www.computerweekly.com/print/ArticlePrinterPage.asp? liArtID=124987&FlavourID=1 (accessed April 18, 2005).
5. Ibid.
6. Ibid.
7. Ibid.
8. *CIO* magazine web site, www.cio.com/awards/watch/index.html (accessed June 21, 2005).
9. John J. Ciulla, "What Is a CIO?" Executive Summaries, *CIO* magazine web site, November 13, 2002, www.cio.com/summaries/role/description/index.html (accessed February 17, 2005).
10. Ibid.
11. Ibid.
12. Ibid.
13. Sisco, "The CIO's First Priority Is to Understand the Business."
14. Richard Pastore, "Staying Out of the Pool," *CIO* magazine (September 15, 2001), www.cio.com/archive/091501/edit.html (accessed April 18, 2005).

15. Ibid.

16. Thomas Wailgum, "The No. 1 Challenge: Managing Expectations," *CIO* magazine (October 1, 2004), www.cio.com/archive/100104/manage.html (accessed April 18, 2005).

17. Ibid.

18. Stephanie Overby, "IT Incorporated," *CIO* magazine (May 1, 2004), www.cio.com/archive/050104/incorporated.html (accessed April 18, 2005).

19. Ibid.

20. Ibid.

21. Ibid.

22. Ibid.

CHAPTER 5

Effective Communication
Skills and Styles

If you don't go after what you want, you'll never have it. If you don't ask, the answer is always no. If you don't step forward, you're always in the same place.

—NORA ROBERTS[1]

BREAK OUT AND COMMUNICATE

Today's CIOs, and presumably tomorrow's, need to have excellent communications skills and other soft non-IT skills to truly be effective as an IT executive leader. Soft skills, which typically include communication, business knowledge, leadership, motivation, and negotiation skills, are increasingly becoming important today as CIOs strive to become more strategic. According to Robert Half Technology, an independent research group and global provider of IT professionals,

> IT people need to have the ability to communicate at the board level. Being able to understand the business needs of an organization and translate that to a technology solution—to me, that's where the rubber meets the road.[2]

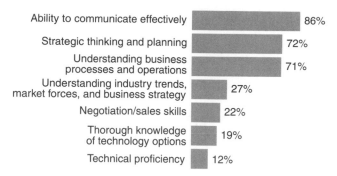

Ability to communicate effectively — 86%
Strategic thinking and planning — 72%
Understanding business processes and operations — 71%
Understanding industry trends, market forces, and business strategy — 27%
Negotiation/sales skills — 22%
Thorough knowledge of technology options — 19%
Technical proficiency — 12%

EXHIBIT 5.I   **The Personal Skills Most Pivotal for Your Success as a CIO**

Source: Used with permission and adapted from *CIO* magazine, October 1, 2004.

According to a Robert Half Technology survey of 1,420 CIOs, the most important soft skills for IT staffers rank as interpersonal skills (37 percent), written or verbal communication skills (20 percent), the ability to work under pressure (17 percent), overall business acumen (11 percent), and professional demeanor (7 percent).[3]

According to the *CIO* magazine State of the CIO 2004 Survey, the ability to communicate effectively was ranked as the number one most

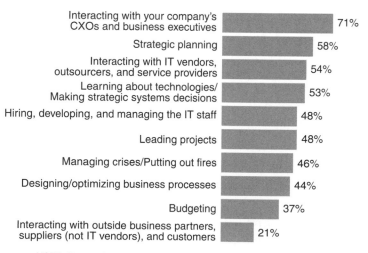

Interacting with your company's CXOs and business executives — 71%
Strategic planning — 58%
Interacting with IT vendors, outsourcers, and service providers — 54%
Learning about technologies/Making strategic systems decisions — 53%
Hiring, developing, and managing the IT staff — 48%
Leading projects — 48%
Managing crises/Putting out fires — 46%
Designing/optimizing business processes — 44%
Budgeting — 37%
Interacting with outside business partners, suppliers (not IT vendors), and customers — 21%

NOTE: Respondents checked all answers that applied.

EXHIBIT 5.2   **How You Spend Your Time**

Source: Used with permission and adapted from *CIO* magazine, October 1, 2004.

important personal skill for successful CIOs, with a response rate of 86 percent.[4] In addition, the *CIO* magazine survey indicated that CIOs spend their time communicating via a variety of ways, including interacting with other CXOs and company executives (71 percent), interacting with vendors (54 percent), hiring, developing, and managing the IT staff (48 percent), and leading projects (48 percent)[5] (see Exhibits 5.1 and 5.2).

I asked a group of world-class CIOs for their opinions on the importance of communication skills in IT leadership positions today.

CIO SURVEY

How important are communications skills for a CIO today?

- 100 percent of respondents indicated that communications skills were *highly important.*
- 0 percent indicated a moderate or low response.

What strategies would you recommend to midlevel professionals today to build the communications skills needed for a CIO position?

Communication comes in many forms, including face-to-face verbal, written, presentation, body language, attitude, videoconference, conference calls, etc. A good CIO needs to at least be effective at all and stellar at one or more. The key to success, however, is to be empathetic and aware of how your communication is being perceived by the recipient. What you thought you sent may not necessarily be what was received. So the strategy is to be aware of all the different communication channels, hone your communication skills for each, understand your strengths and weaknesses, but above all tune in and be perceptive as to how your message is being received.

—John W. Von Stein, Executive Vice President and CIO, The Options Clearing House

Speak in public—they won't really listen to you there, but they like to know you can do it. Practice—find places to exercise this skill. Don't worry, the only people not nervous about this even after years of practice are liars and sociopaths.

—John R. Sullivan, CIO, AARP

Observe colleagues and peers and incorporate their good communication techniques and avoid the bad ones. Look for opportunities to improve your skills via speaking at professional events and forums and writing/publishing technical papers and case studies.

—William Stansbury, Vice President of Software Development,

Target Software

There is one critical strategy for a technology professional to follow— LISTEN! I would also learn to talk without the techie jargon and develop some public speaking skills.

—Earl Monsour, Director, Strategic Information Technologies,

Maricopa Community College District

Make "rounding" an integral part of your routine. If you are not out on the "road," make daily rounds of all or part of your functional areas in a manner where you informally interact with staff. At least once a week, visit/call a customer that is affected by your work area to talk about impact, quality, satisfaction, or future issues.

— Nelson H. Ramos, CIO, IT Strategist, Sutter Health

THINK, WRITE, AND SPEAK

Understanding the business is key to being a successful IT leader/CIO, and building effective relationships helps break down common IT-to-business barriers to obtaining that knowledge. That said, seasoned IT professionals will likely think long and hard about how they build an effective communications *strategy* before implementing one. This typically involves listening to your customers, mapping an IT strategy, and creating a communications plan that fits the *culture* of the organization you are serving. According to *CIO* magazine research, new CIOs should know when to talk and listen:

> The first year should be focused on building empathy. Listen closely, build up goodwill. Then you can start to figure out what needs to be done.[6]

Part of learning the business and communicating effectively is to be available and responsive. An open-door policy and frequent *walk-bys* to IT staff and your business customer's offices can help facilitate unofficial dialog and lines of communication that are based on honest conversations that may yield some trust down the road. When ready, roll with your strategy and get busy talking, listening, and communicating effectively via electronic means. Below are some effective communications techniques used by today's IT leaders.

Written

- Reinforce IT governance and standards via e-mail and on the corporate intranet. Develop a one-stop portal for all IT information on strategies, goals, standards, research, methodologies, presentations, and project templates, and communicate to staff repeatedly. Measure the effectiveness of the draw by reviewing web statistics to ensure that your audience is coming to your site.

- Be responsive to e-mail requests and voice mails. Give honest and factual answers to questions, even if they may be painful to deliver. Where necessary, be available for in-person conversations to explain tough decisions or directions.

- Write and publish IT best practice case studies to showcase some of the good work your organization has done and share information with other professionals.

Speaking

- Communicate IT terms and topics in non-IT speak when dealing with other executives and key decision makers outside of the IT group. Speak in terms that they'll understand to help get your message across and get what you want, whether it be project buy-in or budgetary approval to fund a new project.

- Build effective relationships with key executives and communicate often with them about business strategy, IT policies/governance, and joint projects.

- Ask for feedback from your customers on how IT is performing and whether the IT team is meeting business objectives and challenges. Ask for feedback, then listen.

- Meet frequently with the IT team via *all-hands* meetings to discuss progress on projects, key wins, strategies, and challenges. Communicating a consistent strategy to the IT team is essential to keeping up morale and staying focused on the right tasks.

- Communicate directly to business unit staff, possibly at company-wide or division meetings. Let your customers and staff know what IT is doing to add value to the organization and why. Demonstrate new tools and systems as appropriate, and recognize key project staff publicly for their contributions. Break down IT-speak into layman's terms that are easily understandable by non-IT professionals.

- Speak at external seminars, conferences, and workshops. Doing so accomplishes two things: (1) it develops public speaking skills and (2) promotes IT and your organization as a whole externally.

- As an executive sponsor, engage project teams in meetings to drive results and to communicate ownership and commitment.

Bottom line, IT leaders need to communicate often and in multiple directions to be effective and trusted (see Exhibit 5.3).

I was recently reminded just how important communications skills are to IT executives at a recent annual review of mine. My supervisor pointed

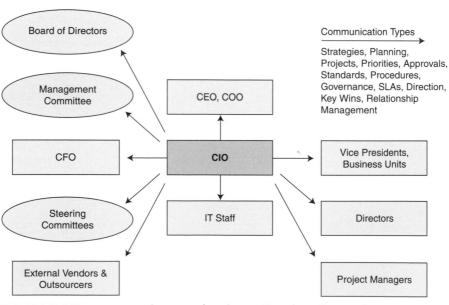

EXHIBIT   5.3   Communications Matrix—Upward, Lateral, Downward, and External Communication

to a 360-degree feedback rating of mine from peers and noted that I needed to stay focused on communicating IT topics and strategies in layman's terms that the business staff could easily understand. And that advice came from a 360-degree rating of 93.4 percent on my communication skills.

In conclusion, a *CIO* magazine research note quoted two sitting IT leaders:

> You can have the most wonderful ideas in the world, but if you can't communicate them, it won't make a difference.[7]—*Margaret Myers, Principal Director for the Deputy CIO with the United States Department of Defense*

> A big part of the CIO job is salesmanship. If CIOs can't communicate, their projects will die—either at the approval stage when the executive committee rejects them, or at the implementation stage when the users resist them.[8]—*Ron Margolis, CIO, University of New Mexico Hospital System*

MANAGING EXPECTATIONS

Managing expectations on what the IT department can accomplish and actually deliver is a key component to an effective communications strategy. Let's face it, staff and budgets are not unlimited, and project request demands of IT usually outpace supply in most organizations. Thus, one of the biggest challenges for CIOs today is other business executives' unrealistic expectations of IT. According to *CIO* magazine's State of the CIO 2004 survey, "respondents cited unrealistic or unknown expectations from the business as the *highest* hurdle to their job effectiveness, trumping inadequate budgets, proving IT's value, and alignment between business goals and IT efforts."[9] The article goes on to suggest several ways to bridge the expectations gap:

1. *Get the IT shop in order.*[10] Signs of an ineffective IT department include unclear IT governance, lack of strategic plans, a history of underdelivered IT projects, possibly over budget, and a lack of consistent processes and methodologies to flesh out business requirements and implement technical solutions.

2. *Listen to your customers* and stop talking at them.[11] Spend an ample amount of time facilitating team discussions and brainstorming sessions with your IT staff that center around business needs and

requirements. Meet with major business unit leads as needed to get feedback on pain points, how IT is doing, and how IT could help address key issues. Some CIOs do this via methodologies and interview processes to gather requirements and feedback. Others actually embed IT staff in the business unit to bridge the IT-business gap. According to a veteran CIO who's spent time at WellPoint Health Networks and embedded IT staffers in each business segment,

> They are the funnel for the needs of that business unit. Those people live with that unit, support that unit, and bring back into our meetings their project needs, their business needs."[12]

Other CIOs use project portfolio management and engage their business leaders in the prioritization of work and projects, which can lead to a more realistic view of what IT and their resources can accomplish.

3. *Educate your customers.*[13] Communicate existing IT projects, goals, and resources to business peers and educate them on the processes used and time to complete certain tasks and projects. Customers need to know that IT is not a *black box* in a vacuum, where requests go in and solutions come out. Simply put, time spent communicating processes, staffing situations, project statuses, and deliverables associated with a methodology informs business users that system solutions don't just appear without hard work, consistent processes, and time. More than likely, they'll understand that it takes time to deliver quality results if explained properly. That said, I'm not projecting that customers will soften and just roll over; they will continue to demand, but will accept realistic events that can help you develop creative solutions that deliver results and build relationships.

4. *Get on the CEO's agenda.*[14] Request to be included in CEO strategy planning meetings and get woven into the business plan. Another approach used by some CIOs is to rename the IT steering committee to the *business planning committee* and include key business unit leaders. Sell the idea that IT needs to be involved in business planning and strategy early on.

5. *Communicate often.*[15] Managing expectations is about proper and timely communication to the right audience. Communicate status updates for any outages frequently, possibly multiple times per day

if the outages are unplanned and large in scope. Some CIOs communicate IT progress and activity via quarterly reports and newsletters to all staff. I think it's safe to say that there is no such thing as overcommunicating as a CIO, especially when critical projects are ongoing and in the event of planned and unplanned outages. Also, it's really important to communicate to non-IT staff in business terms.

Not all communication is verbal or written. Body language, including expressions and gestures, can also be an effective way to communicate. Effective communicators are also cognizant of the potential pitfalls of negative body language and know how and when to use it effectively to communicate the right message. In addition, as stated in previous chapters, alignment of IT with the business is critical to facilitate honest and open lines of communication necessary to deliver results. Simply put, a business-savvy and aligned IT shop needs to communicate often and effectively to properly understand issues, build relationships, and develop and deliver solutions that add value. According to one IT executive at a health-care organization who got engaged early with a business customer, "We had an earlier start on a system than we would have if that strategy had become known to IT later."[16] In another example of effective communication that leads to better collaboration, a CIO created a database to share information across the company that helped produce some great ideas with cost savings of more than $100 million dollars over three years. For example, "a suggestion to use unbleached paper towels led to savings of $40,000 to $50,000 annually."[17]

In conclusion, an important technique to communicate with key stakeholders and better align IT is to track and evaluate the effectiveness of IT policies, processes, staff, and projects. Two simple ways to do this include (1) 360-degree feedback in the review process and (2) annual surveys to key business units to evaluate IT progress and measure perspective outside of IT. Improving how the business units perceive IT can be beneficial for IT and the company as a whole. A recent *CIO* magazine article from a survey of 106 companies selected for their strong reputations in IT noted the following top five benefits of positive perception:

1. Increasing IT credibility

2. Fostering closer alignment between IT and business unit objectives

3. Improving teamwork of joint IT–business unit staff on projects

4. Promoting wiser investments

5. Improving the CIO's ability to influence the business[18]

The article went on to suggest the following top five ways to change negative perception:

1. Ensure business units share in ownership of projects with IT.

2. Conduct strategic planning sessions with business unit leads.

3. Have a solid IT governance process for investing in IT.

4. Present IT wins to key stakeholders, executives, board members, and the company as a whole.

5. Track IT's record on projects for success and lessons learned.[19]

CIO SURVEY

Provide an example of a communications missed opportunity and the consequences that resulted in your career as an IT leader.

I went head to head with a newly hired business manager who I determined was a flake. I was branded as confrontational and aggressive to the new guy and it focused me in a poor light and slowed my inclusion in critical discussions. The new guy turned out to be a flake and left the company. Damage control, however, still took a while.

— *Martin Gomberg, CTO, A&E Television Networks*

In a previous CIO position, I didn't communicate as well as I could have with a regional general manager. As a result, his expectations for a new IT project did not match the reality of what the project intended to accomplish. Although the project team achieved all of their goals, my failure to communicate well with the general manager led to a widespread perception that the project was a failure.

— *Richard C. Belanger, CTO, Target Software/Target Analysis Group, Former CIO, Forrester Research*

Probably the biggest challenge I have ever faced as a green CIO was when I came in to take over an ERP project from the functional unit that had left out IT from the project. They had set expectations very high with the user community in an attempt to get their support and resources for the project. We attempted to adjust the expectations to something more reasonable. However, it took years for the community to catch up with the reality of what could be done after the miscommunications that had occurred prior to my arrival. Moral of the story—communicate often and truthfully, and set reasonable expectations for projects and then exceed them rather than the other way around.

—David G. Swartz, Vice President and CIO, The George
Washington University

COMMUNICATING PROJECT WINS—GIVING CREDIT WHERE CREDIT IS DUE

Part of an effective communications strategy is to communicate key project wins and recognize IT and business unit staff for their accomplishments. In my career, I've made a point to do this frequently and through a variety of channels, namely:

- Demonstrations to staff at all hands meetings, with specific mention of key staff and their contributions.
- E-mail to staff after a successful project launch.
- IT all hands meetings.
- Published articles (IT and business trade magazines) highlighting best practices for successful and creative implementations.
- Awards—I've submitted numerous submissions to *calls for award nominations* over the years to recognize the organization and key staff for significant accomplishments on projects that clearly demonstrate adding IT value to the company.

In conclusion, CIOs must develop and execute on an effective multipronged communications strategy that involves frequent and honest communication in non–IT terms to the mass business audience. With regard to communicating orally, most effective speakers are those that communicate *what they know well*, in laymen's terms if appropriate, and highlight the key points, typically no more than three, for their audience to remember. Those wishing to join the CIO ranks should practice oral and written methods of communication, become very effective and convincing, and do it over and over again.

WHAT DID I DO TO PREPARE?

My communications preparation for the role of CIO started well before my first professional job and well before my undergraduate and graduate course work. I became aware of the value of honest and effective communications skills when I landed my first sales job at 16 years old, selling computer equipment and software in a retail store. It was there that I started to understand the impacts and rewards of solid communication skills. I watched and learned from more seasoned and experienced sales professionals who sold more products. Fast forward to today—I did the following to develop and hone my communications skills over the years:

- I got a mentor or two early in my professional career. They helped guide me on effective methods of communication.
- I practiced and delivered hundreds of presentations to a variety of audiences without any notes.
- I learned from peers and supervisors how to write effective communication and e-mails.
- I published articles and best practice case studies in leading IT publications.
- I watched, listened, and learned from other more seasoned and effective communicators to gain additional skills and techniques that have enabled me to become a better communicator.
- After receiving a technical MBA, I signed on as an adjunct faculty member for a reputable university in the United States. It was there, over nearly a decade, that I honed my communication skills—listening, speaking, and writing. There's no better environment to improve one's skills than among a group of intelligent, inquisitive, and vocal group of graduate students craving more knowledge.

RECOMMENDATIONS

Those wishing to join the ranks of today's CIOs or simply improve upon existing communication skills can do a variety of things to hone their skills. I'd recommend starting with the following:

- Solicit feedback from peers and supervisors on how to improve your communication skills. Don't take constructive criticism personally.

We can all take a tip or two from folks who have exceptional communication skills.

- Get a mentor early in your career who can help you develop effective oral and written skills.

- Join Toastmasters or other groups that offer free advice and techniques to professionals who desire to improve their communication skills or overcome a fear of public speaking.

- Practice oral presentations. In the early years, don't underestimate the importance of the need for a good verbal delivery. Also, make sure that the content of each presentation is suitable for your audience and be aware of the time limits allotted for presentations.

- Communicate on what you know. Effective communicators know their material well, are confident but not cocky, and tailor content toward their audience.

- Publish successful project wins and case studies in IT and business trade magazines.

- Communicate key project wins as appropriate (verbally and in writing) to appropriate audiences.

- Go after some industry awards. If you or your organization is selected for an award, it's a great way to build credibility and recognize key staff for their accomplishments.

- Pursue speaking engagements at conferences and seminars. These forums are great ways to hone your presentation preparation skills as well as oral communication skills. It's also a great way to promote your company and best practices to others in your field and is an excellent way to network with other professionals.

ENDNOTES

1. http://www.chrysaliscreativity.com/category/inspirational-quotations/ (accessed December 9, 2005).

2. Jon Surmacz, "The Hard Truth: Soft Skills Matter," *CIO* magazine (January 15, 2005), www.cio.com/archive/011505/tl_numbers.html (accessed February 17, 2005).

3. Ibid.

4. Edward Prewitt and Lorraine Cosgrove Ware, "State of the CIO 2004 The Survey: It's All About You," *CIO* magazine (October 1, 2004), www.cio.com/archive/100104/survey.html (accessed February 17, 2005).

5. Ibid.

6. Edward Prewitt and Stephanie Overby, *Fundamentals of the CIO Role—The Evolution of the CIO Role* (Framingham, MA: CXO Media, 2003), 12.

7. Ibid., 14.

8. Ibid.

9. Thomas Wailgum, "Managing Expectations," *CIO* magazine (October 1, 2004), www.cio.com/archive/100104/manage.html (accessed February 17, 2005).

10. Ibid.

11. Ibid.

12. Ibid.

13. Ibid.

14. Ibid.

15. Ibid.

16. Victor D. Chase, "How HCA Brought Business, IT Together," *CIO Insight*, July 1, 2002, www.cioinsight.com/print_article2/0,2533,a=28591,00.asp (accessed June 30, 2005).

17. Ibid.

18. Stephanie Overby, "Turning IT Doubters into True Believers," *CIO* magazine (June 1, 2005), 51.

19. Ibid.

PART TWO

Preparing for the Role of the CIO

CHAPTER **6**

What Executive Recruiters Are Looking For

I don't know the key to success, but the key to failure is trying to please everybody.

—Bill Cosby[1]

RECRUITING TRENDS FOR IT EXECUTIVES

If you really want an honest shot at a first-time CIO position, you have to be well prepared to deal with an experienced executive recruiter. You must be well rounded, have great credentials and experience, be able to highlight demonstrated results in prior positions, be *known* in the right circles, and be prepared to strut your stuff in a confident, but not arrogant, way during the interview process. Most CIO and other IT leadership positions are not advertised in local and regional newspapers. They are most often worked through a network of executive recruiting professionals via paid contracts with employers or via an executive level network drawn from a pool of contacts ranging from a group of peers, colleagues, mentors, and vendors. According to a recent in-depth interview with Martha Heller, managing director of IT leadership practice at the Z Resource Group, there are several new trends in executive recruiting for IT professionals today, most notably:

- *More hiring.* The market has definitely been heating up over the past six to nine months. With the U.S. economy improving, companies are getting back into a growth mode, which from the CEO's perspective can mean an opportune time for making a leadership change in the office of the CIO. From the CIO side, that means more open positions and more looking around. Also, many CIOs have been at their companies during four to six years of layoffs, major budget cuts, and outsourcing, and they are tired of the environment and the low morale of their staff. They're ready for something less frustrating, more strategic, more fun, and more lucrative. The *lucrative* part is key. You always hear people say that job changes are more about responsibilities and challenges than income. I don't agree. Compensation comes in at the very top of the list for most candidates these days.[2]

- *Reporting structure changes.* The number of open CIO positions that report to the CEO has been dropping, while the number of CIO positions that report to the CFO is increasing. Our research shows that there are still more CIOs reporting to CEOs than CFOs, but I think we're going to see that level off in the next year or two. This is still fallout from the technology bubble and the continued sense that IT is a cost center that needs to be reigned in.[3]

- *Compensation.* A recent survey from *CIO* magazine shows that the average salary compensation for CIOs is about $180,000 right now, not including bonuses and options, which is down a little from last year. I believe that as the job market continues to heat up and the competition for really good CIO candidates increases, we will see a rise in total compensation over the next few years.[4]

- *Skill sets.* CEOs are looking for that unique combination of technology management experience, strategic business knowledge, great relationship building skills, and the ability to align business and IT. As always, cost containment remains critical to the CIO role, in the CEO's view. That said, most CIOs still come out of IT, nearly 80 percent. The best bet for candidates in distinguishing themselves is to collect and emphasize their business experience. In other words, they need experience in both the tactical and strategic sides of IT, that is, to have had the experience of running major application development or integration projects or managing a data center, but also managing a profit and loss. Global experience is becoming increasingly important as well.[5]

Global and local economic factors always seem to have an impact on the recruiting marketplace. According to an Online Market Intelligence Research Center article, "the single biggest obstacle facing the recruiting industry today is a weak job market."[6] In the United States, "unlike the nation's previous business recession, which lasted from July 1990 to March 1991, job growth has not resumed."[7] International experience is also a great way for CIO candidates to differentiate themselves from other candidates. Executive recruiters today are working harder than ever to fill open executive positions across the globe, and the market drivers in one country can differ greatly from those in another. According to a recent article and interview with the managing partner in Asia for Heidrick & Struggles International, Inc., "there is never enough of the right kind of talent. Whether it's Korea, China, Hong Kong, or Japan, the companies all want the same people: returnees with experience in the Western business world—people who are technically savvy, bilingual, bicultural, and Western-educated, and who can straddle both sides of the fence.[8] That said, trends are important to job candidates today, and anyone looking for the right next IT executive position should recognize relevant trends and understand that they vary greatly depending on a variety of issues such as industry, sector, region, country, and economic climate.

CONTACTING AND WORKING WITH AN EXECUTIVE RECRUITER

The typical process that an executive recruiter goes through in filling a senior position for a client is actually quite simple and consistent. According to Korn/Ferry, a leading international executive search firm, their recruiting process is broken down into the following five simple steps:

1. *Define objectives and specifications.* Work closely with the client to understand their business and culture, position scope, responsibilities, reporting relationship, and profile of the desired candidate.

2. *Identify and assess candidates.* Identify and confirm target sources using our proprietary database and a network of contacts. Identify, evaluate, and screen candidates, including internal ones as appropriate.

3. *Interviews.* Facilitate client interviews, obtain feedback from the client and candidates, conduct reference checks, and prepare detailed profiles and evaluation reports depicting each candidate's strengths and weaknesses.

4. *Select executive.* Conduct finalist interviews, and negotiate salary and benefits.

5. *Follow-up.* Ensure smooth transition and assimilation for the executive and ensure client satisfaction.[9]

So, how and when should CIO candidates approach an executive recruiter as they make their way up the ladder toward an IT executive position? Candidates today can start with submitting an updated and compelling resume. Many executive recruiters today have robust web sites that allow candidates to post their resumes and learn about a subset of search positions that they are conducting. Most often, these firms use the web to collect resumes and build a list of searchable candidates in their database. Not all recruiters agree with this method of finding viable candidates. While many recruiters offer this capability, it often doesn't lead to an onslaught of calls from recruiters once a resume is uploaded. According to a recent interview with the Z Resources Group, that's not what gets the job done.

> Avoid submitting a resume cold. CIO searches are strategic and targeted. The recruiter typically has a specific company and set of candidates in mind before he or she picks up the phone looking for a candidate. The chances that an unsolicited resume matches a client's requirements at any given point in time are incredibly slim. Furthermore, the most attractive candidate is typically *not* looking for a job. Candidates uploading resumes in bulk are almost advertising that "they're on the market," which may not be the message they want to send.[10]

According to the Z Resource Group, there are three great ways to prepare and begin working with an executive recruiter.

1. *Network.* Like almost anything else in business, executive recruiting is all about relationships. So, the old adage, *network, network, network,* is critically important to keep in mind when approaching recruiters. An executive recruiter will fill an open position by targeting a particular company, often designated by the client, and by tapping his or her own network to find candidates whom other CIOs consider

to be first rate. The better known you are in CIO networks—either as a *peer* or as an *up and comer*—the more likely an executive recruiter will learn of you and make contact. So, joining IT leadership forums and attending CIO events should be a mainstay of your professional activities to gain exposure to the right folks.[11]

2. *Get exposure.* Executive recruiters read *Information Week*, *CIO* magazine, and many other publications that list the top 100 or 500 IT leaders. Getting your name on those lists, winning IT leadership awards, and publishing articles in trade magazines are great ways to wind up on an executive recruiter's call list.[12]

3. *Build relationships.* Talk to peers or colleagues about executive recruiters they have enjoyed working with and ask for an introduction. As with sales, referrals are the best entrée into a new relationship. Once you have a relationship with a recruiter, remember that it is a two-way street. Even if the position he or she has open is not right for you, the recruiter will see you as a great source of referrals to other possible candidates. If you can be of value to a recruiter in that respect, he or she will remember you when the right position comes along.[13]

At what point should a CIO candidate approach an executive recruiter? It depends, but a common answer among recruiters is *as candidates become known for their accomplishments*, whether from experience, awards, or publications. Today, most often a sitting CIO will refer up-and coming candidates to executive recruiters for positions that they themselves may not be interested in. Today's CIOs usually stay in touch with a close set of trusted executive recruiters and treat them as part of their core network. According to Martha Heller of the Z Resource Group,

> If I were a senior level IT executive, I would always want to be in touch with a few good recruiters, whether I was actively looking or not. Even if you are content in your current position and *are not on the market*, you should have reliable channels for learning about new positions. As good as your current job is, there may be a better one around the corner.[14]

I find this advice to be very true. In fact, one of the key factors that helped me land my first CIO position was a referral from another respected and well-known CIO. In the past several years, I've personally referred several up-and-coming IT professionals to a series of recruiters. That old adage must be true: network, network, network.

PREPARING FOR A MEETING WITH AN EXECUTIVE RECRUITER AND NEGOTIATING TO WIN

Once you've got a recruiter working in your corner, it's time to prepare for the interview and potentially the negotiation part of the process. First and foremost, candidates need to prepare for the interview and learn about their prospective employer. The more you know about the hiring company and any issues that they may be going through, the better. The following tips may prove helpful in preparing and meeting with an executive recruiter for an IT executive position:

- *Be prepared.* The more information you have on a prospective employer and their industry, the better. Conduct research to learn of any public information and/or issues surrounding the employer and be prepared to discuss them. You can never do too much research on a prospective employer.

- *Focus on your accomplishments.* Give concrete examples of relevant successful projects and leadership from prior positions. Accentuate your strategic skills by highlighting key strategies and results demonstrated. This is your shot. I guarantee that your competition will spend a lot of time on this area during the interview process.

- *Ask questions.* Find out what pressing issues, challenges, and projects are on the docket for the next year and then draw from your experience and accomplishments to explain how your skills and leadership could help them deliver results.

- *Be creative in your responses to key questions.* Don't just give yes or no answers. Your answers to tough questions should be targeted to differentiate you from other candidates.

- *Maintain a positive and confident attitude.* Always stress the positive, never the negative.

- *Always tell the truth.* If there is a gap on your resume that warrants an explanation, be truthful, but brief in your response. If you've recently left an organization, say why and try to put a positive spin on it.

- *Don't negotiate salary during the interview process.* If and when you make it to the final set of candidates, the recruiter will surely discuss salary with you.

- *Don't be overanxious*, regardless of how badly you may want the position.

The initial interview session and first impression you leave with your executive recruiter could make or break your chances to get to the next level of the interviewing process. If a candidate makes a good impression and has the experience and qualifications desired, he or she has a fair shot at speaking with the prospective employer. Keep in mind, recruiters are the first screening to the client, and they'll never recommend a candidate to their client that is weak and unimpressive. Once you get to the employer portion of the interview process, stay cool, calm, and collected and use the same honesty and integrity approach used with the executive recruiter. If you're lucky, you'll end up as one of a few finalists. Then, and only then, do you get to discuss salary and benefits.

SURVEY RESULTS FROM EXECUTIVE RECRUITERS

As part of the research for this book, I surveyed a select group of regional, national, and global executive search firms that specialize in information technology executive recruiting. Representatives from these firms were asked to provide feedback to a dozen questions that were designed to assist prospective CIO candidates and help them prepare for the role of the CIO today. That said, the information presented below is directly from the recruiting pros and is intended to give clear and comprehensive guidance to those seeking to become IT executives and leaders.

RECRUITER SURVEY

What are the top 10 *skills* that CIOs need to have today to be competitive?

A distinguished group of executive recruiters weighed in on this important question. Their results have been compiled and ranked in response from highest to lowest:

- Business acumen and knowledge of a wide range of business areas
- Leadership skills—the ability to create a vision and strategy
- Management skills—the ability to lead and motivate others
- Team-building skills
- A broad technology background
- Excellent interpersonal and general communication skills
- The ability to deliver services to a wide range of customers
- Customer focus
- Global perspective

What advice would you give to *first-time* CIO candidates as part of the recruiting process?

Overprepare. First-time CIOs are often competing against sitting CIOs for a new opportunity. The first-time candidate needs to demonstrate a thorough understanding of the industry and cultural environment by asking insightful questions and having concise and well articulated answers. Step-up candidates (as first-time CIOs are often referred to) will have greater success pursuing CIO opportunities within the same industry. As a result, having credible references from the business, technical, and senior leadership perspective will be very important in helping the company get comfortable with hiring a first-time CIO.

—*Eric J. Sigurdson, Managing Director,*
Russell Reynolds Associates

Know the hiring company's business and industry cold. During the interview, try to relate major business decisions the company has made to an experience you have had. Have a few revenue generating ideas in your pocket to discuss if the situation warrants. Prepare some reasons for your leaving your current position, which are positive and not critical, and relate those reasons directly to the position for which you are interviewing. Do NOT discuss compensation during the interview. If you are a strategic CIO and the company is looking for someone purely tactical, sniff that out during the interview and don't take the job! After the interview, ask yourself some simple questions: Would I like to work for this person? Would I be proud of this company? Are my skills the right fit for this job? If the answer is no to any of them, don't take it! If you are just starting out and don't yet have an interview—network, network, network. It's the best way to learn of good opportunities.

— *Martha Heller, Managing Director, IT Leadership Practice, Z*
Resource Group, Founder of the CIO magazine *Executive Council*

They should be able to speak clearly and succinctly about their accomplishments of note and show the business value and benefit derived from doing those things.

—*Beverley Lieberman, President, Halbrecht Lieberman Associates*

Understand business problems and be able to articulate experience delivering against those problems. They should spend time understanding the client company and the challenges they face and be able to go into meetings (recruiter and client) with insightful and thorough questions.

—*Katherine M. Graham, Principal, Heidrick & Struggles*

I would advise any first-time CIO candidate to come prepared with specific measurable accomplishments (with benefits) they achieved for their prior organizations—specifically how they used IT to increase cost savings and create more efficient processes.

—*Timothy Ward, Senior Consultant, The McCormick Group*

What are the most common gaps between what CEOs/COOs are looking for in a CIO and what a CIO can actually deliver on?

CEOs often want a CIO who is visionary and who is strategic, yet most often they value and emphasize the need for their CIO to work on tactical initiatives. Many CIOs do not feel that they are being tapped for their strategic abilities.

—*Beverley Lieberman, President, Halbrecht Lieberman Associates*

CEOs and COOs hire us to find great CIOs who can understand the business, their strategy, challenges, and opportunities. They want someone who speaks their language and has demonstrated experience in helping solve business problems with the use of technology. More and more companies are using technology as a competitive edge.

—*Katherine M. Graham, Principal, Heidrick & Struggles*

Business process change. A CEO may want his or her CIO to bring the company through a major business model change. However, if the support and messaging are not clear and delivered from the top, the CIO will have an extremely difficult time pushing through the change at the business process level. Most CEOs truly believe that they want to hire a strategic, revenue-generating CIO. However, once on board, the CIO spends all his time putting out fires and never truly gets to the strategic work.

—*Martha Heller, Managing Director,*
IT Leadership Practice, Z Resource Group

I have found the most common gaps to be the following: (1) how long it takes and how much it costs to implement new systems that can help create a competitive edge, and (2) the lack of agreement and consensus around the prioritization of technology-oriented projects.

—Eric J. Sigurdson, Managing Director,
Russell Reynolds Associates

What are the top five areas of experience that CIOs need to have today?

Results from participating executive recruiters are below and have been compiled and ranked in response from highest to lowest:

- Knowledge of the industry and customers of their company
- Prior senior level technology management experience
- A track record in managing large-scale projects
- Vendor and sourcing management
- Strategic planning
- Thorough knowledge of business processes and how to improve them
- The ability to recruit, build, and motivate a team to perform at a high level

How important is consulting experience for a *first-time* CIO and why?

- 17 percent responded with *high.*
- 50 percent responded with *medium.*
- 33 percent responded with *low.*

Most successful CIOs are relatively consultative in their approach to working with business. Whether they have formal experience working for a consulting firm or have a consultative leadership style, they need to become trusted advisors to their internal constituents in order to be successful.

—Eric J. Sigurdson, Managing Director,
Russell Reynolds Associates

Consulting experience can be a great training ground to learn methodologies, processes, and delivery. It isn't necessary if experience in a large company that has formal training programs is in place around these areas. Consulting experience coupled with management positions in leading companies can be a very successful and sought after recipe.

—Katherine M. Graham, Principal, Heidrick & Struggles

CIOs today are taking on more strategic roles within their organizations. It's imperative that a CIO be able to listen to his or her customers and deliver what they need.

—Timothy Ward, Senior Consultant, The McCormick Group

Consulting experience is not critical to a first time CIO; however, the communication and business experience that come along with consulting is. If a first time CIO can gain that experience through P&L management or through working in other functional areas, that's just as valuable as consulting work.

—Martha Heller, Managing Director,
IT Leadership Practice, Z Resource Group

What other ways can first-time CIO candidates differentiate themselves from others and how important is it to do on their resumes versus in the interview process?

Resumes and interviews should communicate what the individual has been able to deliver. Candidates who can prove they are results oriented and delivered against business problems will clearly be viewed as the top percentile.

—Katherine M. Graham, Principal, Heidrick & Struggles

First-time candidates can differentiate themselves on their resumes and in interviews through the following: (1) Tying their IT projects and accomplishments to IT value. How did a major enterprise IT deployment contribute to the company's financial performance? (2) Demonstrating their leadership during a turnaround situation. How did they drive major change while keeping staff morale up, communication lines open, and systems running? (3) Describing the time(s) when they have taken over the CIO's responsibilities temporarily; (4) Describing their participation in enterprisewide committees and their experience working in various disciplines inside of IT. These differentiations are equally important on the resume and in the interview process. Both are critical steps in the recruiting process.

—Martha Heller, Managing Director,
IT Leadership Practice, Z Resource Group

An MBA from a top school and international experience.

—Beverley Lieberman, President, Halbrecht Lieberman Associates

1. Go back to school full or part-time to earn an MBA from a well respected academic institution.
2. Have a respected mentor or reference speak with the hiring manager (or recruiter) early in the search process.

3. Have concrete examples in mind to discuss with the recruiter or interviewer about your past success.
4. Overprepare for your meeting, but only let the knowledge come out through natural conversation.

—Eric J. Sigurdson, Managing Director,
Russell Reynolds Associates

What are the top three most important things that CIO candidates should highlight during the interview process with executive recruiters and potential employers?

- Ability to deliver on promises
- Strong interpersonal skills and a multicultural company
- Knowledge of the hiring company's business and industry
- Proven ability to tie IT accomplishments to IT value
- Strong leadership through a major corporate or business change
- A business partner
- A record of promotion within a company versus job hopping to get the next promotion

How important are financial management skills in becoming a CIO and why?

- 50 percent responded with *high.*
- 33 percent responded with *medium.*
- 17 percent responded with *low.*

It's absolutely critical that a CIO have financial management skills. Technology is becoming one of the largest investments a company is making, and the CIO must understand what they are getting for their money and how it impacts the overall company. Another reason is more and more CIOs are reporting to the CEO or CFO and cost containment is always something that is looked at. If a CIO wants the attention of a CEO or CFO—they better understand the financials of the company and how technology investments play into the overall picture.

—Katherine M. Graham, Principal, Heidrick & Struggles

CIOs manage large budgets and do a lot of vendor contract negotiations. They are expected to run their departments as if they had a P&L.

—Beverley Lieberman, President, Halbrecht Lieberman Associates

More organizations are turning the IT budget controls over to CIOs. A good CIO needs to know how to effectively manage several million dollars. Also, in this Sarbanes-Oxley world, CIOs have to be more aware of how IT plays a role in the corporation's finances.

—Timothy Ward, Senior Consultant, The McCormick Group

Proving IT value and providing bottom line results from IT expenditures are critically important to the CIO role, so a CIO must possess the financial management skills to talk revenue and profit margins with the CFO and line of business heads.

—Martha Heller, Managing Director,
IT Leadership Practice, Z Resource Group

It really depends on the culture of the company. If the position reports to a CFO, it is more important that the CIO have strong financial skills in order to hold their ground in negotiating new projects. In the case where the position reports to the CEO, it still may be helpful for the individual to have outstanding financial skills in order to justify their solution in terms easily understood by the CEO and others on the leadership team.

—Eric J. Sigurdson, Managing Director,
Russell Reynolds Associates

What is the best academic background for the CIO role today and why?
The top three responses from the executive recruiting pool are listed below and are consistent with my expectations:

- A technology/computer science undergraduate degree as well as an MBA
- A quantitative undergraduate degree and an MBA
- An MBA

What is the minimum number of years of work experience that is necessary to be a viable candidate for a CIO role today?
The top three responses from the executive recruiting pool were:

- 15 years
- 12-15 years
- 10 years

I've seen CIOs of leading companies with only 15 years experience and other first time CIOs with 25 years experience. It all depends on what you have been able to accomplish and what value you have brought to the firm/company as a whole. Results speak volumes!

—Katherine M. Graham, Principal, Heidrick & Struggles

The number of years of experience depends on the size and complexity of the organization. In general, the minimum number of years would be 12–15 for a CIO of an organization with revenues in excess of $1 billion dollars. The average years of experience for sitting CIOs in the Fortune 500 is approximately 25 years.

— Eric J. Sigurdson, Managing Director, Russell Reynolds

What career advice would you give to midlevel professionals today to help them prepare for a CIO role in the future?

Spend some time working inside of a business unit, preferably with P&L management experience. Work on your communication/relationship building skills. Find a mentor who is already in the CIO role who can help direct you on your career path. Make networking a critical part of your skill set. Keep a detailed database on the people you've met and the interactions you've had. Networking is by far the most effective way to get your next job.

—Martha Heller, Z Resource Group

Establish a reputation for adding significant value to the organizations you support. Identify mentors early in your career that can help you grow personally and professionally. Take risks early in your career to assume leadership roles for either troubled projects or high risk/high reward projects where you can stretch yourself both personally and professionally. Ensure you are working inside of a corporate culture where your style is a strong match for the business. If you find yourself frustrated or bumping against walls internally, consider changing companies in order to operate in a more synergistic environment.

—Eric J. Sigurdson, Managing Director, Russell Reynolds

Get broad experience in IT and get experience in project management, international assignments, applications development, systems integration, telecommunications, production, and help desk. Also, learn many business functions such as finance, marketing, and supply chain.

—Beverley Lieberman, President, Halbrecht Lieberman Associates

Always understand the big picture and be able to map it back to your individual contributions.

—Katherine M. Graham, Principal, Heidrick & Struggles

What percentage of CIOs are hired from within their existing company?

The responses from each executive recruiter is listed below:

- 30 percent—Halbrecht Lieberman Associates
- 25 percent—Heidrick & Struggles
- Less than 20 percent—Z Resource Group
- 50 percent—Russell Reynolds Associates
- 50 percent—The McCormick Group

WHAT DID I DO TO PREPARE?

I've had great success in working with executive recruiting firms to date. Earlier in my career and in an attempt to position myself for the job that would lead to a CIO role, I directly contacted a few executive recruiting firms and started putting my resume, accomplishments, and experience in circulation and in their databases. In preparation for my first CIO assignment and through a decade of preparing, I selected employers and positions with top organizations in a variety of business sectors to gain broad business and IT exposure that had more responsibility than previously, to be able to show demonstrated increases. During this time, I landed a senior technical position with one of the largest nonprofit organizations in the world, where I headed up software development, e-business, database management, and internal business. While at the AARP and working with the CIO, I helped develop an IT strategy for applications development, which included the use of IT standards, methodologies, and proposals that resulted in solutions and systems that were developed to help our customers. In addition, I also embarked on several strategies to greatly reduce operating costs while improving the technical environment. During this time, I continued to teach and stay current on a variety of technology topics by serving as an adjunct faculty member at The Johns Hopkins University graduate school.

In addition to making contacts with executive recruiting firms and focusing on building a portfolio of results, I continued to publish best practice case studies in a variety of technical magazines over a span of about 8 years. The exposure gained in national and international technology magazines led to several speaking opportunities at a variety of information technology conferences and other IT venues. As appropriate, I updated my resume at the various executive recruiting firms and maintained contact with them to let them know how my career was progressing. Shortly thereafter, a top global recruiting firm contacted me to see if I was interested in applying for a newly opened CIO position. The trigger for this contact was not the result of my preliminary work with a variety of executive recruiters, but the result of being referred by an existing CIO that was familiar with my work ethic, consistency in results, and skills. That said, preparation for working with executive recruiters is important, but contacts in your network may be more important in gaining access to a reputable recruiting firm.

RECOMMENDATIONS

To close this chapter out, I advise professionals aspiring to become CIOs to not lose focus on building the right resume of accomplishments and increasing levels of responsibility that may lead to running a world-class IT organization. The following recommendations are designed to help candidates prepare for working with a reputable executive recruiting firm to land their dream job:

- As your career matures, start contacting a variety of local and regional executive recruiting firms to get your accomplishments and aspirations known. Where available, publish and update your resume as necessary in online recruiting databases.

- Focus on accomplishments and tying IT best practices that solve business-related problems that can be measured and perceived by your customers.

- Make an effort to publish best practice projects and/or IT strategies that have produced results. Publishing articles is an excellent way to raise your profile and get recognized as an IT leader. It also looks great for the organization that you're working for by putting their name on a best practice and successful project or strategy.

- Where appropriate, apply for awards that can raise your exposure. Documentation required to submit for an award can often be time consuming. Thus, select your award categories carefully and take the necessary time to submit a solid application. Awards are great ways for staff and organizations to be recognized for achieving excellent results. They often also lead to speaking engagements, which again raise the exposure level that most executive recruiters are looking for.

- Get some international experience if possible. Top consulting firms offer an excellent opportunity to gain great experience with international clients.

- As recommended by several CIOs and the distinguished set of executive recruiters, consider getting an MBA to complement a solid technical set of skills. CIOs that have MBAs are often more exposed to the business side of an organization, while managing the technology to achieve business objectives and goals. They are also on more even footing with other executives, who usually have MBAs as well.

- Continue building your network. This is one of the most important recommendations that I can give to CIO candidates. When the time is right for you to apply for a lead IT executive position, you'll likely have a number of avenues through which to pursue it. Make sure that your portfolio of accomplishments is complete and compelling, or you may not be able to successfully compete with other candidates. My grandfather once told me that it's *"who you know to get in the door and what you know to stay and succeed."*

ENDNOTES

1. Bill Cosby, www.famous-quotes-and-quotations.com/success-quotes.html (accessed June 3, 2005).
2. Interview with Martha Heller, Z Resource Group, conducted June 1, 2005.
3. Ibid.
4. Ibid.
5. Ibid.
6. Brian P. Lee, "Executive Search 2003: State of the Industry Report" (Hunt-Scanlon), July 31, 2003, www.hunt-scanlon.com/research/esi_report.htm (accessed May 27, 2005).
7. Ibid.
8. "Focus on Leadership Trends in Asia—An Interview with L. Kevin Kelly," http://www.heidrick.com/NR/rdonlyres/548A226B-F393-4DD5-93DE-0DFD52F56C5C/0/HS_Leadership_Trends_Asia.pdf (date accessed May 25, 2005).
9. Korn/Ferry International web site, "Search process," www.kornferry.com/Library/Process.asp?P=SearchProcess (accessed June 2, 2005).
10. Interview with Martha Heller.
11. Ibid.
12. Ibid.
13. Ibid.
14. Ibid.

CHAPTER 7

Building the Right Network

Nothing great was ever achieved without enthusiasm.
—RALPH WALDO EMERSON[1]

DEVELOP YOUR TECHNOLOGY AND BUSINESS NETWORK EARLY

If you really want an honest shot at a first-time CIO position or even a better and more challenging CIO job, then you'd better value your network! Like a well-positioned real estate location, your *network, network, network* will more than likely be one of the most important sources of inspiration, contacts, guidance, mentors, advice, and, yes, references for that perfect career position. My grandfather told me a long time ago that "it's who you know to get in the door and what you know to stay." That said, professionals today should start planning to build their network early and make sure that they spend an ample amount of time nurturing and growing it. I have personally found building and growing my network to be one of the more important aspects of managing my career.

Just what is a network? As I've researched for this text, I've learned that it means a lot of different things to different people. According to an Itsnotwhatyouknow.com article, "career networking is meeting people and building relationships to assist educational planning and reach career goals" and typically starts sometime between high school and college.[2] The article goes on to suggest that career networking can provide invaluable assistance to a career at any stage, even for an established professional.[3] According to About.com, "business networking is the process of establishing a mutually beneficial relationship with other business people and potential clients and/or customers."[4] Some take the concept of networking to a level that can be financially quantified. According to the chairman of Ecademy.com, a web site and company dedicated to connecting business professionals, "It is my belief that you need 1,000 people in your network for each £100,000 you wish to earn each year."[5] The author goes on to suggest that the actual worth of each person in your network is £100 per annum.[6] I could go on quoting numerous articles and research surrounding the topic and benefits of the business network, but I won't and the reason is simple. A *network* to me is more than just about my career and job advancement and conducting business. It's about sharing information, experiences, conducting business, and having fun with people that I trust and like (see Exhibit 7.1). My network as a professional and *person* today, simply put, includes the following:

- *Friends.* My friends often provide some of the most honest feedback to questions that I ask them along with insights that might not normally be shared via a typical professional relationship.

- *Peers in my career field.* I often ask for feedback, input, and advice on technology issues, strategies, and challenges. Contacts with peer individuals can be made via associations or forums like conferences, speaking engagements, peers in other organizations, academic institutions, and past and current employees.

- *Professionals outside of the IT field.* Professionals outside of the information technology field, but often related or integrated, are also an important part of my network. These individuals include, but are not limited to, professionals with expertise in accounting and financial management, contracts, business process, sales and marketing, and law.

- *Mentors.* Some of the most important people in my network have been a select few mentors that have helped guide my career as well as given me great advice when asked and needed. These individuals include a small group of prior supervisors as well as some respected business professionals with whom I did not have a formal reporting relationship.

- *Vendors and consultants.* In the information technology profession, it is damn near impossible to be successful without the help of some key and strategic vendors and consultants. Vendor/consulting contacts that develop into trusted relationships and even personal friends are even more important to me and are surely part of my expanded network, even if I change jobs or positions. Several of my network contacts in this arena fall outside of information technology and for a simple reason—*not everything revolves around IT.*

- *Recruiters.* At some point, most professionals moving up the IT ladder will need to work with an executive recruiter or specialist, especially since many of the top IT jobs are not recruited in the same fashion that lower and midlevel positions are. IT professionals should start adding recruiters into their network as they pass into mid-level IT management positions.

- *Prospective employers.* Networking with professionals from other organizations also helps broaden and develop one's network. Relationships made with key individuals from other organizations can sometimes lead to sharing best practice information, war stories, or even a tip toward a future employment opportunity. That said, people are what make a network strong, and communicating, socializing, and establishing relationships with other professionals can be beneficial to both parties.

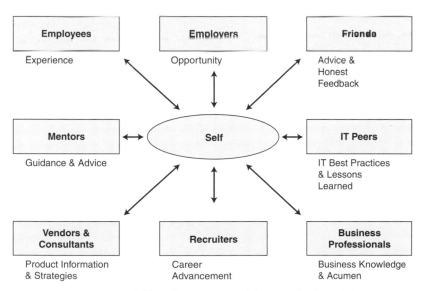

E X H I B I T   7 . I   **Effective Networking Relationships**

What is the right time to start building a network? My answer: before your first job. If you think about it, most informal networking starts very early in life, usually with friends and teachers during adolescence. Some teachers become mentors, while other early friends may end up being moved outside of the *inner* circle as people change and mature. As most grow older and into young adults, they often change their definition and parameters of what they consider to be a network. As young adults gain additional knowledge, some on the job, others via formal education, their network also evolves to include people from a variety of contacts and institutions.

I asked my group of CIOs their thoughts on the importance of a network. Their answers are below and consistent with my expectations.

CIO SURVEY

How important is it to build an effective network in the quest for a CIO appointment?

- 74 percent responded with *high.*
- 21 percent responded with *medium.*
- 0 percent responded with *low.*
- 5 percent did not respond.

Some additional comments from select members are listed below. A senior level appointment needs an effective network.

—*Earl Monsour, Director, Strategic Information Technologies,*
Maricopa Community College District

I would think that requirement would be high and I would depend on that *today* if I needed it. It is, however, not how I found my path into the CIO position.

—*Martin Gomberg, CTO, A&E Television Networks*

What are the top five benefits of networking for you today?

1. A network of trusted professionals can provide advice and feedback where necessary.
2. Saves time, energy, and money.
3. Learn about new technologies, ideas, and best practices for implementing solutions.
4. Job opportunities.
5. Honest references on vendors and products.

Honorable mentions from CIO feedback include the following:

- Leads to talented individuals that you may need to recruit
- Facilitates faster learning
- Improves credibility of IT with board members, the CEO, and other business executives
- Social interaction/golf

WHERE DO CONSULTANTS AND VENDORS FIT IN?

As an ex-management and technical consultant, I believe that consultants are right up there in importance with my staff and business customers. In Chapter 8, the section titled *Partnerships—The Key to Success* goes into depth on the need and skills required for today's CIOs when it comes to managing vendors, along with the products and solutions that they provide. Simply put, I believe that consultants fill a key role in the development of a broad array of information technology support, including, but not limited to

- IT strategy and planning.
- advisory input and research to products and solutions.
- purchasing assistance and other IT-related consulting services.
- process and change management expertise.
- hardware support and service.
- software implementation and project management support.
- training.

I typically tend to use consulting resources for short-term engagements and prefer to leverage outside expertise and/or support for projects and systems that fall outside of my staff's expertise or scope. Other CIOs that I know and network with use a combination of short-, long-, and midrange services from small to large consulting firms to augment their staff skills and/or manage demand for projects.

A CIO's consulting strategy is clearly an individual preference with both pros and cons, but facts are facts—not many organizations that I've seen, worked with, or consulted for take a *go it alone* approach and don't rely on consultants for some type of work. As a result, consultants should be a key part of one's network. Over my career, I've typically kept close ties to really effective consultants, even if they've changed firms, and have leveraged them as necessary in various organizations that I've worked for. A trusted relationship with an impartial, fair, and knowledgeable consulting partner can be a really good thing and yield positive results for both parties.

FIND A SOLID MENTOR

Mentors are usually really special people who have great insight, solid experience to draw from, a broad set of professional and personal contacts, and are bright, energetic, and giving in their time and advice. Good ones are also extremely *rare* and hard to find. I've been fortunate in my career to find a few mid- and senior-level professionals who have served as mentors to me, and who helped guide and develop my technical and business skills.

My first mentor was fairly early in my professional career when I was in my mid-twenties. She was a mid- to senior-level consulting manager who had exceptional client management, project management, and communication skills. For some reason, she decided to take me under her wing and help guide my career, possibly because I was always very energized and positive about working with our customers and solving their problems. She helped guide me in developing and honing my client management and communications skills. This was one of the most important boosts for my career at the time. Back then as with today, being technical or having business acumen was not enough to be put into a leading and *customer-facing* position with a client or prospective customer. Communication skills, polish, presentation style, and other soft skills are just as important as hard technical skills in today's IT market. I remember many instances of practicing presentations with her until she was satisfied that it would be done and delivered right. Her advice still stands in my memory today: *Present on what you know and target the script to your audience.*

My second and third mentors were also ex-consultants, but served as executives within organizations where I also worked. Both were knowledgeable and influential. After developing a closer professional relationship with them, I started to have more open and honest conversation on a variety of topics ranging from skill development, business knowledge, and even personal issues. What I found as an indirect result of my closer association with these two mentors was that I learned most by observing them in a professional environment. Expanding that to observe others in action, I learned additionally what *to do* and infrequently what *not to do* by watching them and other executives and visionaries in leadership roles. When I wanted clarification on something, *I asked for it,* and since we had established a trusted relationship, the information and conversations usually flowed freely in both directions. That said, I believe that human beings learn in one of three ways: (1) preparing for the task at hand, doing the research, spending time on a well thought out approach for a project or product, and yielding a successful outcome; (2) watching someone else make a mistake; or (3) making the mistake themselves. I prefer the first and second option. Finding a professional mentor that can influence and advise directly or indirectly, with intent, is as important as all of the other professional and career development one might attempt to gain rolled up into one powerful and effective package.

So, how does one find a mentor? For starters, ask for help from someone who is influential, knowledgeable, reputable, and interested in you, and that you think you can build a long-term relationship with. Some people searching for mentors simply get lucky. According to an *Inc.* magazine article, Kent Sutherland did just that over 20 years ago when he talked his way into Sam Walton's office, and hasn't stopped relying on the visionary's advice since.[7] According to the *Inc.* magazine article, Sutherland met Walton on his third visit to Wal-Mart as a supplier, and over the next several years "Walton would grant Sutherland brief, intermittent audiences, in which he would take the younger man aside and they'd talk business, like coach and quarterback crafting a game plan."[8] All of my mentors to date have been at a higher level in experience and seniority. I think that this is important since mentors should have refined skills and deep experience that mentees most likely don't have, but desire. Additional mechanisms that may lead to finding a good mentor include the following:

- Networking with professionals beyond your current grade or level—inside and out of your current organization. Exposure is key to meeting the right mentor.

- When you find someone that you respect and think you can learn from, ask for guidance.

- Academic environments are great places to search for a mentor, especially since colleges and universities are geared toward higher learning and helping students grow.

- Search out organizations and programs that offer mentoring services. Some are free, while others are fee based.

- Look at management training programs within your organization and apply for ones that increase your interaction with senior management executives. Some companies have well-defined programs to mentor new executives or rising stars. During my tenure at a Fortune 200 financial services firm, I went through an excellent 20-month senior management training program, and the experience and executive level contacts made were invaluable.

According to an *Inc.* magazine article, it usually takes some research and time to identify *multiple* candidates for mentors.[9] According to Kathy Kram, an associate professor of organizational behavior at Boston University School of Management and author of *Mentoring at Work*, "I think people really ought to think in terms of multiple mentors instead of just one."[10] Kram goes on to suggest that not all mentors need to be executives that are high ranking. She adds, "Peers can be an excellent source of mentorship."[11] In a different *Inc.* magazine article, the author suggests the following steps to finding a great mentor:

- *Know yourself.* Think about where you are and where you want to be.

- *Be proactive.* Develop a plan and ask before waiting to be asked. Also, get your ducks in a row and do some research before you start lobbing dumb questions to a prospective mentor. Smart people (and mentor candidates) don't like stupid questions and tend to cater to individuals that crave answers to the right questions that have sound motivations.

- *Ask for referrals.* Friends and colleagues can be a great source.

- *Keep an open mind regarding who your mentor might be.* A mentor doesn't necessarily need to be a heavy hitter or power player. They do need to be knowledgeable and have a desire to help others, specifically in the traits and skills you may want to improve.

- *Identify alternative mentors*. Never put all your eggs in one basket. Mentors can come from a variety of places, both business and non-business related.

- *Know what you want to achieve from the relationship.*

- *Think about people who have been your mentors in the past*.[12] We've all had mentors in our lives whether we realize it or not. Review the experiences, pros, and cons, and apply what worked or was valuable in the past going forward.

Interestingly, mentors that I've run into over my career (both mine and those of others) usually also had a mentor or several in their lives and appear to be eager to pay it forward. That said, I've adopted the *pay it forward* strategy as well and currently have at least two mentees that I've been working with to help develop their skills and careers. It's quite rewarding and I highly recommend that sitting CIOs and other executives give it a try.

DON'T IGNORE YOUR STAFF

Current and ex-staff members are a great source to include in one's network. Over my career, I have kept in contact with a group of what I would consider the *best and brightest* technology and business staff members that served in one capacity or another, either under my direction or working on projects together. These resources, usually trusted colleagues and possibly even friends, are an excellent pool of professionals that I've put into my network of contacts. I keep in touch with ex-employees, provide advice to them as requested, and ask for their input on a variety of topics, including technical information and tips, business trends, related projects, and strategies that they may be working on. Interestingly enough, I'm serving as a mentor to at least one of my ex-subordinates.

GREAT FORUMS FOR NETWORKING

Networking is all about meeting new people and building trusted relationships. That said, there are a number of venues and opportunities today for

IT and other professionals to meet, share information and ideas, and build business and potentially personal relationships. I surveyed a group of CIOs to get their opinion on their favorite and preferred networking venues today.

CIO SURVEY

List the top five networking forums that you use today?
The top five most common answers include the following:

1. Informal networking with friends and peers
2. CIO/peer executive events and councils
3. Participation on advisory boards or via board of director positions
4. Meetings and discussions with vendors
5. IT advisory meetings and/or conferences

The full set of answers that I received were so forthcoming and valuable that I have to list beyond the top five. The honorable mentions include the following:

• Golf events and tournaments
• Former employees, co-workers
• Technology user groups
• Online networking services
• Professional associations

According to the CareerJournal.com, the Wall Street Journal's executive career web site, social networking web sites (Friendster, LinkedIn, etc.) have become popular lately and provide a simple forum for networking in a virtual world.[13] The CareerJournal.com article goes on to suggest that "it isn't what contacts can do for you: it's what you can do for contacts," and that being a *rainmaker* while online is important for business networking.[14]

In closing, I asked my CIO group to give advice on how to build an effective network. Their creative and honest answers are listed next.

What advice would you give to a professional wanting to become a CIO regarding building effective networks?

Some of the best answers are provided below.

Focus on being a good CIO instead of being a good politician first. You have to have some successes from which to develop further professionally.

> —*Shyam K. Dunna, CIO/Assistant General Manager, MARTA*
> *(Metropolitan Atlanta Rapid Transit Authority)*

Get out and talk with people. Share your ideas with people through formal and informal settings. Listen to what they have to say and show interest. Build relationships and nurture them.

> —*David G. Swartz, Vice President and CIO,*
> *The George Washington University*

It's a must— in our field, when you are experiencing problems with software implementations, as an example, usually no one else in the executive ranks of your company can help you. You have to rely on your contacts for advice or their experiences. I don't think you can be a successful "CIO in a vacuum."

> —*Carol F. Knouse, Senior Vice President and CIO,*
> *The Donna Karan Company LLC*

Being a raging extrovert helps! If not, then leverage industry conferences and clubs. Educate yourself on relationship management techniques, complex sales techniques, and social etiquette (it amazes me how poor most people are at even basic table manners and social graces). You not only have to know people, but you have to get them to like you and want to do things for you or the contact is for naught. Do favors for people and help them be successful in whatever is important to them.

> —*John W. Von Stein, Executive Vice President*
> *and CIO, The Options Clearing Corporation*

Build your network in a targeted way to achieve a set of short- and long-term objectives, constantly revisiting the currency, quality, and depth of your relationships.

> —*Mykolas Rambus, CIO, W.P. Carey*

WHAT DID I DO TO PREPARE?

I started building my network long ago. During my undergraduate college days, I pursued an opportunity to gain some experience through a cooperative education program. The co-op program provided me an opportunity to gain some *on the job* experience for credit while still in school studying computer science and business. It was on the job that I first saw the value of developing a professional network. After eight months of full-time job experience and the contacts made, I started to map out a plan for a more expansive network. On an interesting note, I received one of my first full-time job offers after graduating college as a result of the contacts made during my cooperative work experience.

In the business world and as I grew into increasingly more expansive and management positions, I continued to build my network to include friends, vendors, other IT and business professionals, and academic advisors/ professors. After completing graduate school and through my association with the academic community, I met and developed relationships with several knowledgeable and influential people from multiple universities. Shortly thereafter and as my career and publishing progressed, I was offered and accepted a position to teach as an adjunct faculty member at the graduate degree level at The Johns Hopkins University, my graduate alma matter. Today, I continue to network both inside my organization and with a variety of people in other organizations in an effort to share ideas, best practices, knowledge, and information. I utilize many of the same forums described by my CIO survey group to communicate with peers and other professionals. Thus, my network is not one-way. I often help others with advice that they seek from me. I firmly believe that the effort that one puts into networking and the contacts made will only enhance both parties and provide a great opportunity to learn, grow, and succeed in life and business.

RECOMMENDATIONS

To close this chapter, I recommend the following to anyone wishing to become successful in business, life, or even in the pursuit of a world-class CIO or other executive level position:

- Get out and network today! Build, grow, and feed your professional network. If you don't have one, develop a plan for establishing and/or growing your network. Seek out other seasoned professionals for advice on developing a network.

- Check out some of the popular social online networking forums like LinkedIn and Friendster. Make sure to pay attention to published best practices for online etiquette.

- Integrate key vendors and consultants into your network. Work with vendors and account executives to learn the details of their products and service offerings. Vendors should be a key part of one's professional network.

- Take a look at some of the well-respected professional associations and determine if they fit into your networking strategy and plan.

- Look for and find a mentor that can help guide your career and improve your skills.

- Seek out networking forums inside and outside of your professional area of expertise. Some of the more valuable contacts I've made have been outside of the IT field.

- Attend conferences and seminars to meet new people and learn of IT best practice products and solutions.

- Join a users group or an IT council to share information and knowledge.

- Publish best practices and project wins where appropriate to recognize key staff and to expand your network to include the publishing world.

- Volunteer to speak at forums where you have some expertise on the topics being covered and can demonstrate results delivered on a recent project or implementation. Case studies are a great way to build a win-win for your career and your employer's reputation.

ENDNOTES

1. http://www.quotationspage.com/quote/29687.html (accessed December 10, 2005).

2. "What is Career Networking?" Itsnotwhatyouknow.com web site, www.itsnot whatyouknow.com/CareerNetworking.aspx (accessed August 2, 2005).

3. Ibid.

4. Susan Ward, "Business Networking," About.com web site, sbinfocanada.about
.com/cs/marketing/g/busnetworking.htm (accessed August 2, 2005).

5. Thomas Power, "Guru Comment October 2002—Why I Network," Ecademy
.com web site, October 31, 2002, ecademy.com/node.php?id=2869 (accessed
August 2, 2005).

6. Ibid.

7. Edward O. Welles, "The Mentors," *Inc.* magazine (June 1998), pf.inc.com/
magazine/19980601/943.html (accessed August 18, 2005).

8. Ibid.

9. Karen Dillon, "Finding the Right Mentor for You," *Inc.* magazine (October
2000), pf.inc.com/articles/2000/10/14859.html (accessed August 18, 2005).

10. Ibid.

11. Ibid.

12. Jamie Walters, "Seven Tips for Finding a Great Mentor," *Inc.* magazine (April
2001), pf.inc.com/articles/2001/04/22407.html (accessed August 18, 2005).

13. Krista Bradford, "Business Networking Online Can Advance Your Career,"
CareerJournal.com web site, http://www.careerjournal.com/columnists/
perspective/20041025-fmp.html (accessed August 2, 2005).

14. Ibid.

CHAPTER 8

Vendor and Sports Management

Setting an example is not the main means of influencing others, it is the only means.

—ALBERT EINSTEIN[1]

PARTNERSHIPS—THE KEY TO SUCCESS

Managing vendors is a key function in the role of the CIO. Information technology is usually one of the top departments in any organization in terms of employing the most vendors and partners. These partnerships are usually for product support/maintenance, outsourced systems or functions, or consultancy engagements for process improvement and/or system implementations. As an example, typical IT infrastructure (routers, switches, servers, operating systems, databases, etc.) are all usually manufactured and supported by external vendors, some for a fee, while others are freeware or open source. Key application programs that support and drive the business typically run on top of the IT infrastructure and platforms and usually consist of a combination of commercially purchased and custom-developed software. But even the custom-developed solutions usually have some cost associated with the development tools. Outside of labor and training costs, for-fee software development tools and application server software usually involve a capital purchase, plus annual maintenance for upgrades and support. Nothing is truly free, and if it's part of the IT environment, it more than likely has a set of vendors behind the products that help keep IT running smoothly. That said, vendors touch almost every facet of IT today and must be managed accordingly to ensure that the IT department and team can properly support, maintain, and grow the technical environment and applications in support of the business.

Today, the IT vendor market is consolidating, and only the biggest and fastest-growing vendors will survive. Technology mergers over the past few years are increasing the growth and market share of the largest technology players and putting the squeeze on smaller firms that don't make the acquisition or merger cut. According to a recent Tekrati research news report,

> AMR Research expects the top five vendors in 2005—SAP, Oracle, Sage Group, Microsoft, and SSA Global—to account for 72% of ERP vendors' total revenue. The top five vendors in 1999—J.D. Edwards, Baan, Oracle, PeopleSoft, and SAP—accounted for 59% of the ERP industry's revenue.[2]

The Tekrati research article goes on to report that the enterprise resource planning (ERP) application market had solid growth that was impacted by a consolidating software market, where only the strong will get stronger.[3] A 2005 press release on storage spending from IDC, a premier global provider of advisory services and events for the information technology and telecommunications industries, indicated that the top five vendors (EMC, Hewlett Packard, IBM, Hitachi, and Dell) collectively increased their market share from Q1 2004 to Q1 2005.[4] The article went on to indicate that all other storage vendors combined in the period measured decreased market share from 34.6 percent to 32.4 percent.[5] Merger activity in the past couple of years has reinforced the assertion that the IT marketplace is consolidating and putting clear pressure on smaller and innovative firms so that they'll either grow on their own and gain market share, get acquired by one of the big boys, or be forced out of the competitive marketplace altogether. In addition, the past few years have brought large tier-1 vendors together to create mega-companies, putting even more market share and growth pressure on smaller firms. Recent merger examples include EMC/Legato, Symantec/Veritas, and Oracle/PeopleSoft.

Today's CIOs and key IT subordinates spend a tremendous amount of time evaluating and selecting vendors, negotiating contracts, and managing vendors that support their business unit. According to a 2003 Forrester Research IDEABYTE research note, organizations are becoming more sophisticated in their vendor management approach, and taking the following steps to improve their performance:

- *Reducing the number of overall vendors.* Organizations are consolidating duplicate and overlapping services from vendors and consolidating to fewer and more strategic partners.

- *Distinguishing strategic vendors from commodity-based ones.* Strategic vendors, such as key consultancy firms and sales supportive ERP vendors, are more likely to provide benefits that can be perceived by the business and not just by the IT department. These are the vendors with whom IT will likely develop *partnerships* and close relationships. All other vendors that provide an IT commodity such as a device, service, or component, will likely still be IT vendors, just not key or *strategic* ones to the business where value can be perceived outside of IT.

- *Reducing vendor management complexity.* By reducing the number of vendors—strategic and commodity-based, internal, and outsourced— IT shops can reduce the management overhead (typically 3 to 6 percent of a total engagement) and save both time and money.[6]

- *Increasing the number of departments involved in vendor management.*[7] More recent due diligence in vendor management includes time for strategy, sourcing, terms negotiations, contracts, and service level agreements (SLAs) for support, billing, scoring, and vendor management. Thus, more departments than ever outside of IT are now getting engaged and will in some way have an impact toward the management of IT vendors, from legal to contracts and other business units.

The trend in how organizations are managing vendors is changing how IT is adapting to those changes and managing their own vendors and partners. According to a Forrester Research Best Practices research note, collaborative decisions between IT and business units has dramatically increased from 45 percent in 1999 to 87 percent in 2002 as a result of changes in strategy and tasks surrounding vendor management and IT governance (see Exhibit 8.1).[8] So, what are the key vendor management functions that CIOs are adopting today? Forrester Research states that they include

- defining the sourcing strategy.
- contract negotiation and management.
- consulting management.
- service-level agreements and charge-back management.[9]

Skills required by CIOs and their IT staff that manage vendors are absolutely critical today and usually fall outside of the typical IT skill set toolbox, but now include

- excellent communications skills.
- strong contract negotiation skills.
- knowledge of SLAs and best practice service-level approaches.
- knowledge of sourcing options and pricing.
- understanding of financial issues associated with implementation options like application service providers (ASPs), and those that are outsourced, purchased and capitalized, or expensed.

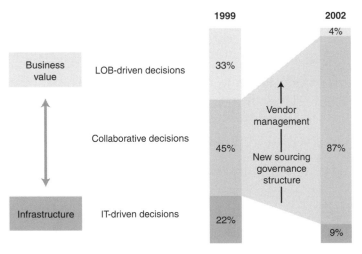

EXHIBIT 8.1

Source: Used with permission from Forrester Research, "Best Practices: Building the Vendor Management Function," March 15, 2004.

- experience with software and licensing agreements.
- vendor relationship management skills.
- contract management.
- charge-back approaches.

Successful vendor management staff aren't necessarily experts in all of these functions, but likely have good knowledge of each requirement or skill set and leverage other professionals inside the organization, including those in legal, contracts, procurement, and finance/accounting departments, and solicit advice as needed from other IT professionals. Thus, today's IT leaders and executives must be savvy in skills that fall outside of core IT skills and knowledge. They must learn to *think like the business* and *act like IT professionals* to solve problems and challenges in the most cost-effective way.

MEASURING PERFORMANCE

Best practice companies with a defined vendor management (VM) function use metrics and other techniques to define and measure performance and effectiveness within their own departments and, if possible, across the entire organization. Some include their vendors, especially key strategic vendors, and partners in the analysis to ensure that business strategy and financial performance are on target. There are a variety of methods to measure performance. Two will be highlighted in this text: (1) corporate performance management (CPM) and (2) the balanced scorecard. According to a recent *Baseline* magazine article, CPM was initiated by companies themselves and is a term for "systems that monitor the key metrics of business performance."[10] The *Baseline* magazine article goes on to suggest that the typical CPM commercial software suite contains modules to "plan initiatives, track progress and analyze the results."[11] Tier-1 vendors that offer this capability today include SAS, Cognos, and Hyperion Solutions. *Baseline* magazine goes on to outline four key steps in the CPM cycle:

1. *Plan.* Develop strategy and metrics. Example: reduce the budget by 4 percent to allow for product price reductions to match competitive offers.

2. *Manage.* Create goals for business units and determine how to achieve them.

3. *Monitor.* Analyze metrics via a methodology such as Six Sigma or activity-based costing.

4. *Adjust.* Alter strategy, goals, and metrics as necessary.[12]

According to *Baseline* magazine, CPM is better than just using a balanced scorecard or Six Sigma alone, since it attempts to ensure that metrics from an initial plan flow smoothly and allow for a more flexible monitoring and analysis process.[13]

The balanced scorecard is an excellent way for organizations and IT shops to keep track of their *wins* and *losses.* According to a *CIO* magazine report on IT value,

> The Balanced Scorecard method links business strategy with financial performance. Implementing it within IT will foster alignment with the business and eliminate projects of little strategic value.[14]

According to the Balanced Scorecard Institute, the balanced scorecard was developed in the early 1990s by Dr. Robert Kaplan and Dr. David Norton, and many companies have benefited from its use over the past decade.[15] The Institute goes on to define the scorecard as "a management system that enables organizations to clarify their vision and strategy and translate them into action."[16] The Balanced Scorecard Institute article recommends that an organization view its performance from the following four perspectives, and then develop metrics, collect data, and analyze performance against those perspectives:

1. Learning and growth

2. Business process

3. Customer

4. Financial[17]

Mobil Oil (now Exxon Mobil) leapt from last to first in profits within the oil sector in the mid-1990s, and Cigna Insurance turned around $1 million dollar a day losses in the early 1990s to a top quartile of profitability within two years and in 1998 spun off a multi-billion dollar division as part of its turnaround.[18] Both of these companies attribute part of their success to the balanced scorecard.[19] There is a debate going on currently as to whether the balanced scorecard can be effective in the IT department alone versus deployed across the enterprise. I'd like to weigh in on this a bit. I think that the balanced scorecard is an extremely effective tool that can have a profound effect on organizations that implement it—with the right support. In order to implement the balanced scorecard across the organization, you'll need key support outside of IT, possibly all the way to the office of the CEO to guarantee participation and use throughout all departments. While there can be significant gains (performance and financial), the sell job to get a balanced scorecard implemented in a small to midsize organization is a challenge. Larger organizations may have an easier time selling the approach, especially if they stress the economies of scale and performance gains that are easier to push through with large IT budgets. Simply put, the balanced scorecard requires money, commitment across business lines, and a balanced scorecard *czar* to help ensure and monitor a successful implementation.

That said, the most financial and overreaching benefits of the balanced scorecard come from an implementation across the entire company. According to a *CIO* magazine article,

> A fully implemented Scorecard cascades from the top levels of a company all the way down. Ultimately, each member of the organization works off a personal Scorecard, striving to achieve personal objectives based on measurements directly linked to the corporate strategy.[20]

So, can the balanced scorecard really have an impact in IT if the CIO can't get buy-in across the enterprise? I believe that the answer is yes. I've implemented a *technology scorecard* in my career and have recently expanded it to include scoring vendors against *defined* information technology and business objectives. There are some hurdles in this *going it alone* approach or implementing the scorecard only within IT. According to *CIO* magazine,

> Installing a Balanced Scorecard within IT is a challenge. It changes the job approach of all employees—not to mention how they're evaluated. CIOs need to take a number of necessary steps to properly lay the groundwork for a successful implementation.[21]

The *CIO* magazine article goes on to suggest four simple ways to mitigate the risk of an *IT-only* scorecard:

1. Prepare the organization for change.
2. Devise the right metrics.

3. Get buy-in at all levels.

4. Plan to follow through to completion.[22]

Metrics are a key part of the balanced scorecard. Understanding the IT and the business drivers could amount to a make-or-break success. According to the *CIO* magazine article, the Hilton Hotel Corporation implemented a successful scorecard strategy that focused on the following major categories: (1) financial performance, (2) customer service, (3) efficient business processes, (4) innovation, (5) learning, and (6) growth.[23] A New Jersey energy company spent some time identifying the right metrics and the right number of metrics to track progress and improvement. Rick Fidler, CIO of FirstEnergy and Senior Process Analyst Mel Brinkman, devised the following three key metrics for success:

1. Percentage of projects completed on time and on budget

2. Percentage of projects released to the customer by the agreed-upon delivery date

3. Client satisfaction as indicated by customer surveys completed at the end of a project[24]

The only way to know if your balanced scorecard approach is working is to measure the results. According to Susan Dallas, research director at Gartner, the best way to tell if your scorecard is working is "if you set higher measurement goals every year and continue to meet them."[25] In implementing an IT and vendor scorecard, I've learned that if you set goals and metrics tied to business objectives, it's easier to develop an IT plan that meets those goals. Expanding the scorecard to key vendors has also proven helpful in identifying key areas for improvements as well as things that our *partners* do well. I believe that recognition, where appropriate, along with honest feedback for areas of improvement, yields the best results inside and out. That said, I rely on honest, straightforward communication to my staff, to my customers, and to my vendors to ensure that we and they all know what is important at the end of the day. Without that knowledge and feedback, I'm not sure that I could appropriately execute my duties as a CIO today.

I asked my CIO survey group how they thought about vendors. Their answers are straight from the pros: Differentiate vendors from partners and offer some key advice to other CIOs and first-time CIO candidates on how to execute the vendor management function.

How do you view your vendors and why? (Outsourcers, partners, just vendors, etc.)

I spend a lot of time up front developing partnerships with our key vendors. If I can trust a partner as opposed to continuously having to manage every detail of a vendor transaction, it will save me a lot of time and effort. The word *trust* is the key. Also, we both have to have some skin in the game—if one benefits, we both benefit, and vice versa.

> —*Earl Monsour, Director, Strategic Planning Information*
> *Technologies, Maricopa Community College District*

10 percent are outsourcers, 10 percent are partners, 80 percent are vendors. Outsourcers and partners provide additional value. Most only supply me with a commodity/strictly price.

> —*Ray Barnard, Vice President and CIO, Fluor Corporation*

If you don't feel that your vendor is a partner, then you have the wrong vendor. Some people take pride in beating up vendors to drive down pricing. I believe you get what you pay for. Of course, negotiation is important, but your vendors are entitled to a profit.

> —*Carol F. Knouse, Senior Vice President and CIO,*
> *The Donna Karan Company LLC*

Most are transactional in nature (price and terms), although some are more important to us than others (IBM. EMC, etc.), so we have a much closer relationship with them, but not up to *partner* status.

> —*John Von Stein, Senior Vice President*
> *and CIO, The Options Clearing House*

We have a group of vendors we refer to as *strategic vendors*. They are more like partners, but never really a true partner. We have a strategic relationship management process that we implement for each of the strategic vendors. IT and Procurement work together to manager these relationships, with one of my direct reports being responsible for the relationship.

> —*Jerry B. Hale, CIO and Vice President of Information*
> *Technology, Eastman Chemical Company*

First, I want to say that all vendors want to be strategic partners. In reality, it depends based on what services they provide, how they provide them and how much I perceive I can trust them to look out for my interests. All vendors start as vendors. If they can prove they can execute, they may become outsourcers to me if their offers are right. Only firms that meet the previous criteria and demonstrate staying power, trustworthiness, and an ability to deliver have a hope of being a partner.

—John R. Sullivan, CIO, AARP

We have a small number of vendors who are considered strategic partners, and the remainder are still key to our IT and business success. Any vendor who is *just a vendor* is not worth our business, especially given the number of companies willing to go above and beyond for our needs.

—Mykolas Rambus, CIO, W.P. Carey

Key vendors I view as *partners*, others I'm up front as far as the relationship basis (value-added, price-driven, service-driven).

—Nelson H. Ramos, CIO, IT Strategist, Sutter Health

Do you scorecard your key vendors to improve performance?
- 18 percent responded with *yes.*
- 82 percent responded with *no.*

We keep precise details on performance, non-conformance and raise these issues with the vendor if applicable. We have received outstanding response/support accordingly.

—John Von Stein, Senior Vice President and CIO,
The Options Clearing House

If so, how often?
Of the respondents that answered *yes* to the previous question,

- 50 percent responded with *quarterly.*
- 50 percent responded with *annually.*

I've recently initiated an annual vendor survey for our *key vendors* in an effort to document deficiencies, score them against our IT business plan and objectives, and set a course of action to improve any issues. It's not a fully implemented balanced scorecard approach, but it does identify key issues of performance that can be traced back to objectives tied to business goals and performance plans. I've found a formal and consistent process that includes key vendors to be valuable in improving performance across the board.

KNOWING WHEN TO OUTSOURCE

Outsourcing is a hot topic in today's information technology space as well as other business areas as business and senior executives look for ways to cut costs. The simple phrase itself is often misunderstood by professionals from business staffers to IT managers and even executives. According to the *American Heritage Dictionary of the English Language*, the word *outsource* is described as "to send out (work, for example) to an outside provider or manufacturer in order to cut costs."[26] WordNet describes it as to "obtain goods or services from an outside supplier; to contract work out; many companies outsource and hire consultants in order to maintain a flexible workforce."[27] Outsourcing is a common practice in IT today, and IT executives have gotten better at evaluating the options for moving work outside of the organization. The intent of briefly discussing outsourcing in this text is simple—it happens in most organizations today in some fashion and there are clearly pros, cons, and best practices to establishing good IT outsourcing strategies. Usually driven by the desire to reduce costs, some companies have over-outsourced their IT environment without properly weighing the pros and cons, and have suffered unanticipated technical outages, reliability of support, or problems with customer support that have impacted IT and the CIO as a whole. There are several types of outsourcing options used by technology professionals today. Some common examples include the following:

1. Fully outsourcing a technical infrastructure component or function such as an *IT help desk, call center, web site hosting,* or even a *data center* to a facility that is owned or leased by another company.

2. Partially outsourcing a function of the IT infrastructure, but within the corporate domain. Examples include *managed firewall services* for devices that sit in your company's data center, *managed application services* for an application that runs on servers in your data center, and *intrusion detection/penetration testing* against your technical infrastructure.

3. Outsourcing application development and maintenance of a software program.

4. Outsourcing the design, development, and manufacturing of a hardware component such as a *networking device, server component,* or

disk system, possibly used in support of a manufactured product or solution.

5. Outsourcing the hosting, care, and maintenance of an application program used by a company, regardless of whether the application was purchased or leased. This strategy, commonly referred to as an *ASP,* is becoming more popular as CIOs look to simplify their IT infrastructure and disaster recovery plans, by hosting the care and feeding of their critical applications outside of their data centers. An example would include hosting an Oracle Financials system at an Oracle hosting partner, where all technical interfaces, hosting of the application, application upgrades, and patch management are done by the commercial ASP vendor.

I've personally used options 1, 2, 3, and 5 in my career as an IT professional. In addition to the *types* of outsourcing solutions, there are a variety of geographic locations where the actual work is performed. The most common solutions involve (1) within the country outsourcing and (2) offshore (out of country) outsourcing. Several countries have recently made significant inroads and become major players in the IT offshore outsourcing business. They include, but are not limited to, India, China, Singapore, Malaysia, and Russia. Today, new and controversial options for geographic location of outsourcing partners are springing up in the strangest places. According to a recent *Network World* magazine article, a new venture called SeaCode

> will place software engineers and application developers on a cruise ship off the coast of California, where they supposedly will have a competitive advantage over more remote outsourcers in India, China and elsewhere.[28]

Today's IT leaders are getting so much pressure to cut costs, while maintaining customer service and satisfaction levels, that they are willing to look at just about any option on the table. The fine balance today is to achieve cost cutting, while maintaining brand reputation, customer support, and reliability. Not all outsourced solutions can deliver these kinds of results, and some are just as strapped for qualified and skilled workers as the organizations that employ them. The *Network World* magazine article goes on to note that "many offshore outsourcers use temporary workers who have little incentive to provide reliable, quality services."[29]

THE SECRET TO OUTSOURCING SUCCESS

According to a *CIO Insight* article, 70 percent of CIOs surveyed said that their companies used some form of outsourcing and that 55 percent responded that their primary motivation to do so was due to a lack of internal resources.[30] The *CIO Insight* article goes on to suggest four simple ways to improve the performance and success of technology work that is outsourced:

1. Identify exactly what work you want done.

2. Communicate your needs clearly to your vendor in contracts.

3. Spend time and clarify SLAs to ensure that both IT work and business objectives are identified along with any penalties for failed performance.

4. Manage your vendor and relationship.[31]

Without proper management of your vendor, contracted inside or outsourced, you're likely to have complications. CIOs and IT departments that tend to have problems with outsource providers tend to make mistakes by (1) failing on due diligence while researching and selecting their vendors, (2) failing to identify exactly what the business needs are and what they want the vendor to do, (3) not clearly spelling out, in contractual terms, the work and SLAs to be performed, and (4) not managing the vendor as they would their internal IT staff.

Not all IT problems will be solved by an outsourced solution, regardless of what the board of directors and other executives may think. Many of them have read newspaper and magazine articles trumpeting the cost-cutting benefits of going offshore, but not that many have read more in-depth research and case studies surrounding IT best practices on consulting and outsourcing. That said, CIOs today need to know when and how hard to push back on board and executive level influence to outsource IT functions simply to save a buck. According to a recent *CIO* magazine article, Stan Lepeak, vice president with Gartner Group suggests that

> [CIOs] need to understand where outsourcing makes sense, rather than be reactive and have it thrust upon them by undereducated business executives. The majority of successful offshore work is still the airtight project that doesn't require collaboration.[32]

Thus, picking the right job to outsource is just as key as picking the right firm. According to the Information Technology Association of America, over 104,000 IT jobs moved offshore between 2000 and 2003, and recent data suggest that the trend will only increase.[33] Work that seems well suited for outsource providers, just to name a few, includes (1) pure application programming/software development that doesn't require a lot of collaboration, but has well documented design specifications; (2) call centers with multilingual staffers; (3) hardware manufacturing with firms that have solid quality control and skilled, but affordable, labor forces; (4) ASPs that understand the intricacies of business applications and support; and (5) pure play hosting solutions where the telecommunications infrastructure is reliable and bandwidth is inexpensive. According to *CIO* magazine, work that is likely to stay in-house includes (1) process mapping, (2) data modeling, and (3) application design.[34] I'd add to that list anything that improves quality, delivery, and a competitive advantage that can be done to reduce the time to market or production of a system between the business unit and IT, emphasizing the need for near instantaneous feedback and interaction between groups of professionals. Thus, collaborative and creative work that requires time-sensitive and confidential interaction among teams within similar geographic time zones is best suited for in-house or near-house solutions. According to an Executive Coach article by *CIO* magazine, outsourced applications that are behind the scenes may make more sense to outsource than ones that are exposed to customers:

> Outsourcing and packages are not the issue. For many companies, outsourcing is a viable solution to address the challenges of small-scale, headcount constraints and legacy IT capabilities. Likewise, packaged solutions make sense if they allow your organization to operate its non-customer facing activities in a cost-effective manner.[35]

In closing, I've never seen an IT organization or department that doesn't rely on an external vendor for products and service. Vendor management is one of the areas that is consuming more and more time for CIOs and IT professionals today, especially since organizations are being pushed to move and conduct work in the most affordable manner, which includes purchased solutions and products, using consultants for difficult and sometimes key technical and business engagements, and pushing work out the door to economical and reliable outsourced providers. Organizations and

CIOs that fail to recognize the importance and overhead associated with vendor management will simply fail and have short-lived IT careers. *We all need somebody to lean on*—whether it is our internal staff or vendors for solutions and support.

INTEGRATING SPORTS TO BUILD RELATIONSHIPS AND GROW YOUR NETWORK

As an introduction to this section, I'd like to go on record by stating that I have increased and expanded my professional network and even my circle of friends as a result of integrating sports into my professional life. In addition, and more importantly with regard to vendor management and performance, I've gotten better results and improved relationships with key and strategic vendors and suppliers as a result of integrating sports into my business life. Getting out of the office to have longer and sometimes more meaningful conversations about business goals, strategies, and pricing has its benefits that extend beyond a constrained 30-minute meeting in a conference room/office or a one-hour lunch or dinner appointment. I've played a lot of sports in my life, but my sport of choice for business is simple—*golf*, and for the following reasons:

- First and foremost, I love the outdoors, and golf provides an opportunity to take in some breathtaking views and get out of the office to think and play.

- There seems to be an endless supply of golf courses and venues with beautiful landscapes that are also challenging for even the most competitive golfers.

- I can learn a lot about a person when I have time to spend with them in a semi-business environment where we can mix business and pleasure. Within a short period of time on the course, I can usually answer questions like "Can I trust them?" or "Do I think we can have a viable working relationship?" In the end, a successful relationship with a vendor comes down to several factors: (1) product effectiveness, (2) service/support, (3) beneficial agreement terms and SLAs, and (4) trust. Sporting events help to break down barriers where one can peer into the crystal ball and retrieve some of that key information.

- Other sporting events and venues simply don't offer the benefits of time, beauty, *participation*, and skill that golf does. While I enjoy an occasional baseball, basketball, and football game, the venues and stadiums pretty much all look the same and I don't get any exercise for the time spent. A pristine golf course, either at sunrise at the start of a round or at sunset finishing up, offers some breathtaking views and challenging holes where bonding with others can occur more naturally.

I don't mix golf and business often, but when I do, I attempt to take advantage of the time spent by discussing business challenges, IT issues and strategies, vendor solutions and pricing, timing for upgrades, and vendor options that are coming down the pike that could benefit my organization. Playing golf allows me to spend quality time with key vendor/partner counterparts in a less stressful environment where we can still discuss business. That said, golf is the de facto sport of business today. I asked a group of CIO experts their thoughts on *mixing sports and business,* and quite frankly I was surprised at some of the low results. Reason being, the majority of vendors I talked to consistently use sporting venues to increase interaction with customers and prospects, drive more sales, and improve relationships with customers. That said, one side may be holding back information and I think it's the CIO community for fear of perception from peers and other executives.

CIO SURVEY

Do you integrate 'sports venues' to build relationships with key vendors?

- 41 percent responded with *yes.*
- 59 percent responded with *no.*

Some additional comments from select panel members are listed below.

[Yes] to build relationships. I also believe in reciprocity or going Dutch.
—*Earl Monsour, Director, Strategic Information Technologies,*
Maricopa Community College District

[No]. I am the customer and would be on the receiving end. I don't typically accept invitations from vendors, especially early on in a relationship.
—*Carol F. Knouse, Senior Vice President and CIO,*
The Donna Karan Company LLC

[Sometimes]. On a rare occasion, I will attend a local basketball or hockey game, and perhaps in the future I will forgive major league baseball and go to one of those games. Based on the number of invitations I get to play golf, a lot of activity must happen out there. . . .

—John R. Sullivan, CIO, AARP

If so, which sports (golf, tennis, football, basketball, baseball, etc.)?
The preferred sports for those that completed this question in the survey include the following, from most preferred to least:

- 85 percent indicated *golf.*
- Tied for second, 42 percent responded with *basketball.*
- 42 percent responded with *baseball.*
- 14 percent indicated *football.*
- 14 percent indicated *hockey.*

Golf—It is still the required game for business.

—Mykolas Rambus, CIO, W.P. Carey

Do you use sporting events/venues to specifically negotiate deals and/or contracts?
Of the respondents that answered the initial question,

- 33 percent responded with *yes.*
- 67 percent responded with *no.*

[Yes]. Where else can you get 4–5 hours away from the office to focus on what we can do for each other.

—Hans Keller, CTO, National Aquarium in Baltimore

[Not likely]. I specifically avoid using events like this to negotiate. I may use them to establish points in a negotiation, but I have never attended an event to close a deal. I have used an appearance of a vendor's executive to express what items must be in or out of a contract to make the deal work.

—John R. Sullivan, CIO, AARP

If so, what percentage of contracts negotiated have been made at vendor-sponsored sporting events?
Of the respondents that answered *yes* to integrating sports with vendors,

- 15 percent was the *lowest* response.
- 35 percent was the *highest response.*
- 25 percent was the *average* response.

HOW MUCH BUSINESS IS DONE OUT OF THE OFFICE?

How much business is done out of the office and especially at sporting events? Apparently more than ever these days. More and more companies on the sell side of the business equation are recognizing the clear benefits of mixing business with sports, and most have been doing it for quite a long time. According to a recent *Washington Post* article, more and more companies are hiring a new breed of consultants to teach their staff how to mix business with sports.[36] According to workplace consultant and business golf expert Hilary Bruggen, who is often hired to teach clients how golf can be an important tool for business, she notes that

> [people who don't play are] choosing to neglect the best business development there is. Many of our clients do business on the golf course.[37]

Bruggen also stresses *not* to "force the business discussion" on a customer or perspective client and *not* to complain about an errant or bad shot.[38] Bruggen also advises women who engage in golf to not get too caught up in the fashion moment and dress outside of the normally accepted sports look.[39] I've been golfing for 25 years and have been on the course when a woman arrives dressed to kill (or dances like, say, Gwen Stafani), which may be best suited for another forum. On the contrary, if any players show up to have fun, keep play moving, but dress the part, it is ok if they can't play; and congratulations—they're part of a well-established club of casual and not-so-good business golfers. Thus, business golf is not just about scoring low and looking good, but having fun and creating a relaxing environment in which to discuss family, friends, interests, and, yes, possibly business. In a business setting, golf is about having fun, establishing a meaningful dialog, and sometimes humbling yourself on shots that accentuate just how difficult the sport can be. The *Washington Post* article goes on to suggest that golf is no longer just a sport for business executives, but rather an "important strategic tool for midlevel management looking to advance, and even for business students whose careers are just starting."[40]

So, just how much business is done on the golf course? According to a Starwood Hotels/Guideline Research and Consulting nationwide survey of 401 business and organization executives who play golf, 63 percent of women and 43 percent of men indicated that they made the biggest sale while on the course.[41] Other interesting statistics from the Starwood study include that

- 13 percent of women and 21 percent of men indicated that they would let a client win.

- 69 percent of women and 87 percent of men indicated that they bet on the course.

- 88 percent of women and 82 percent of men indicated that they cheated.

- women golfers average 30 rounds per year, while men average 46.[42]

Men have known for decades that golf is the sport of business. Today, more and more women are joining those ranks and challenging what used to be the boys club on the course and getting into the action. According to WomenWhoNetwork.com, "businesswomen are using the game businessmen did before them—for networking, for entertaining clients, and for making business deals right on the links."[43] I for one applaud more women on the golf course. It's about time that we moved beyond the days of men dominating the course with bad check pants, silly hats, and bad habits. To be perfectly honest, I believe that men tend to dress better, act more appropriately, and uphold the tenets of golf if there *are* women playing on the course. Today, women that focus on the game and spend time getting better at the sport are becoming more commonplace in tournaments, where normally only good male golfers have prevailed. The WomenWhoNetwork .com article goes on to suggest that golf may matter off the course as well.

> Betty, an American Express executive, played with confidence in a company tournament. The decision-makers took notice—she knows playing in that tournament was a contributing factor for her promotion to executive vice president.[44]

Golf has become the primary *international* sport for business today, especially in countries that are actively participating in the global economy and the IT revolution. I've traveled all over the world and have experienced a lot of things from cultural awareness, beautiful geographic landscapes, and, yes, even golf courses in the least expected places. One of my most memorable times on a course came when I was afforded the opportunity to play three of nine holes in the Kingdom of Bhutan. After traveling through the night and working all day, I got my shot to hit a few balls on one of the highest golf courses in the world. The air was thin and I was using loaner clubs, but the scenery was fantastic! I ended the short round with a great drive that seemed to hang forever in the mountain air. That moment cemented the impression in my mind of just how golf has had an impact across the globe.

An article on the bsicorp.net web site confirmed my suspicions of how the game of golf has moved across the globe and impacted businesses worldwide. The bsicorp article talked about an American executive who had traveled to Japan to solidify a contract for his company and that he learned a thing or two with regard to other customs and especially how they valued golf as a business tool.[45] After several rounds of golf with his Japanese counterpart and no formal business meetings since he arrived in Tokyo:

> When his host suggested another game the next day, the American blurted out in frustration, "But when are we going to start doing business?" His host, taken aback, responded, "But we *have* been doing business!"[46]

The story reminded me just how important it was to understand and respect other cultures when doing business and that business best practices clearly integrate into social gatherings and sporting events like golf. Not fully understanding and respecting other traditions and cultures can kill a business deal before it even gets off the ground. Thus, those who travel internationally for business must do their homework and know what to expect on and off the course.

I believe that the better the golfer you are (with the right attitude), the more successful you'll be on the course from a business perspective and the better you'll sleep at night if you're really competitive. That, of course, is the Holy Grail of business golf, and I for one have been chasing a single-digit handicap for years, only to come up short every year by a few numbers. Not many amateurs play like Tiger Woods, have a great personality, and have solid business skills. Being better does have its advantages, however. Better golfers often get invited to premium events, tournaments, and other social gatherings by *other good golfers,* because, simply put, good golfers like to play with other good golfers, especially if they are competing as a team. Average golfers are just fine for a normal business outing if they have the right attitude and are trying to have fun. Bad or average golfers with the wrong attitude can make an event seem arduous and almost never ending to a golfer with more skill. That said, here's my advice to the business professional and executive of the 21st century who wants to mix golf and business:

- Get out and learn the game of golf. It's the *preferred* sport of business.

- Try to improve your skills to the point where you're having fun and being asked to attend special tournaments to *complement* other members of a foursome.

- Whether you're good or not, have fun on the course, don't get frustrated, and be humble where appropriate. Nobody likes a bad loser at any rank. If you're not getting better with time, just have fun and don't worry about the score. Learn golf etiquette, however, so that you know the right things to do on the course, such as when to pick up and how not to impact another golfer's game. A bad or even average golfer at a business event with a bad attitude is, simply put, a *liability*.

Most business golfers don't break below the score of 100 on a normal round, and the majority of casual golfers are in this pool of statistics, regardless of the new technology on the market.[47] According to the *New York Times*, they offer the following five simple tips for business hosts to succeed in golf and business:

1. Never talk business on the first tee. Save it for later if at all, and let the customer drive the business discussion.

2. Make a simple wager on the match. It keeps the game interesting and often helps build out-of-office *partners* on the course.

3. Don't give any unsolicited golf tips, especially to a prospect or existing customer.

4. Pay for caddie fees where appropriate.

5. Talk business after the round on the 19th hole and avoid heading directly to the parking lot. Business discussions are more natural after a fun and relaxing round.[48]

Golf etiquette and protocol is quite important for a business round on the course as well, regardless of one's skills. Thus, it is just as important to know the rules for mixing business and sport as well as the protocol within that sport. Common protocols in golf include:

- Winners take honors on the tee.
- After the tee shot, the farthest golfer from the hole hits first.
- Don't talk during another person's swing or putt.
- Don't walk across another person's putting line to the hole.
- Fix your ball mark on the green and mark your ball if others are putting first.
- Be ready to play *ready golf* if other groups are pressing behind you.
- Pick up your ball if you've reached a lot of strokes (say triple bogey) and are holding up play for others.
- Replace divots and cover with the provided fertilizer mix if necessary.
- Rake the bunkers when finished in the sand.
- Turn off or minimize the use of cell phones and personal digital assistants (PDAs) while on the course.

According to a *BusinessWeek online Golf Digest* article, "when you're playing golf in a business setting—whether with employees, partners, or customers—man, you'd better be hypersensitive about how you act."[49] Many new golfers sometimes forget to rake a sand trap or replace divots. On a nice course, this is a big mistake. The *BusinessWeek Golf Digest* article goes on to suggest that "if you carry that attitude, especially to a nice private club, it would be easy for the person who has brought you to lose respect."[50] Also, many golfers like to put a mild wager on the game, and there is no shortage of betting games for golfers today. That said, most business experts recommend not betting too much to where it takes away from the bonding and partnering process. In closing, I think that *CIO* magazine summed up nicely the need for today's CIOs to understand the etiquette of golf:

> Golf outings are as integral to the corporate life as board meetings, annual reviews and holiday parties. And if CIOs want to play along, they have to know the subtle points of the game—not necessarily the rules or basic playing techniques but how to behave on the course and avoid perpetrating the cardinal sins of golfing etiquette.[51]

THE VENDOR RESPONSE

As part of the research for this chapter, I also asked a series of vendors, informally and formally, their preference and intent for integrating sports with customers and prospects. The results were consistent and antici-pated—an overwhelming *yes*. Some of the more interesting and honest responses to a series of questions are listed below.

VENDOR SURVEY

Do you integrate 'sports venues' to build relationships with key cus-tomers?

I do incorporate sports venues to build relationships with my exist-ing customers and prospective customers. In today's world of enter-prise software, it is harder and harder to differentiate your value proposition based on traditional dimensions such as technological advantage. Given that phenomenon and the fact that the enterprise software market is becoming more commoditized, the solution for keeping customers and acquiring new customers is through building and nurturing long-term sustainable partnerships. Sporting venues offer an excellent mechanism for enabling this environment. Executives today are extremely competitive and strive to gain competitive advantage in unique ways. Sporting venues enable a very relaxed environment that allows people to develop personal relationships, while still enabling the competitive edge. Personal relationships are critical, in my opinion, because they help provide a mechanism for resolution of issues in the business environment, if they occur. For example, if I develop a relationship with a CEO of a prospective cus-tomer and we are having difficulties in the negotiation of our agree-ment, I have a platform and relationship for resolving these issues based on the interpersonal relationships I developed participating in the sporting event. Executives are extremely competitive in today's marketplace. They have to be. Competition is fierce, and the winners will be on the cutting edge. Sporting venues allow for this natural extension of creating a competitive edge, while enabling the creation of long-term, sustainable partnerships.

—Kyle Bowker, President and CEO, Nextance Inc.

Yes. After 2 decades of selling, one basic truth has been proven time and time again: people buy from people, and usually from people they either like or trust. You can build relationships faster out of the office than you ever could otherwise. Further, sporting events are social—it shifts a potential customer's perception of you away from just being a vendor. The relationship moves to a more personal level, built on shared experience and usually good times. The best manager I ever had said that he did not distinguish between his personal and business life. To him they are unbreakably linked. He also was the most successful sales person I have ever known.

—Michael S. Macey, Sales Director, Netezza Corporation

Yes. I find that sporting events are an excellent way to get to know your customers because those events are typically in a more casual atmosphere that promotes good conversation. Naturally everyone in the group is more relaxed and the conversation isn't forced. This is important because customers are more likely to share information and be more candid if they are in a comfortable setting.

—Daniel M. Jubb, Account Executive,
Hyperion Solutions Corporation

Whenever possible. The main reason is purely to try and build a relationship beyond the contractor/customer relationship. It is my opinion that the vast majority of vendors and contractors are honest people that genuinely want to solve a problem. Having an open relationship with my customers makes it easier to ask difficult questions and trust the answers that I am given. When I truly understand the problem, I can solve it.

—David Brooks, Director of Sales,
Geographic Information Services Inc.

I absolutely integrate golf and sales. Where else can you get the ear of an executive for over four hours?

—Ben Cronin, Account Executive,
Ceridian Human Resource Solutions

If so, which sports (golf, tennis, football, basketball, baseball, etc.)?
Golf is always the best in my opinion. It is hard to get a potential customer to allocate the 5 hours to play, but it is very worth the effort. How many meetings, dinners, etc. would it take for you to get 5+ hours of dedicated time with a prospect? Further, golf is great in that you simply cannot hide your personality on the course. Example: Does he/she get frustrated easily? Do they play really "safe" shots? Does the person always "go for it" no matter the situation? Do they cheat?

—Michael S. Macey, Sales Director, Netezza Corporation

Golf is my game of choice for building relationships. In fact, in a recent conversation with a client from a local country club, he said, "Why would you play tennis? You are across the court from each other, separated by a net!" Golf is key. I guess you could go to a baseball game, but watching a sporting event and participating in one are two completely different experiences. When you take a business meeting from the office to the golf course, the conversation becomes much more personal. In other words, it allows everyone to lower their guard. Getting to this personal level is imperative to building an open relationship. Conversing about life, business, family, sports, etc. allows you to understand a client's personal wins. Add the personal wins to the client's needs and you have a solid foundation of a sound sales process and the building blocks of a long-term partnership.

—Ben Cronin, Account Executive,
Ceridian Human Resource Solutions

Golf is one of the best sports to incorporate into business. You have 4–5 hours of quality time to spend with a prospect or customer. In golf, you aren't fighting crowd noise or other game type distractions, so you have more opportunity to socialize. Many of my senior level customers enjoy golfing and are more likely to take your call if you can invite them to a golf outing. It's a great way to break the ice and potentially develop long lasting relationships. With golf, though, as in any sport, you do have to be careful not to become overly competitive. I am a very competitive person, who hates to lose. If you become too competitive too early in your relationship with a prospect, then that can be a problem. Sometimes I have to remind myself of this point. Baseball games are also an excellent way to get to know your customers for many of the same reasons. The games tend to be a bit more low key than football and the weather is usually better suited for this purpose.

—Daniel M. Jubb, Account Executive,
Hyperion Solutions Corporation

Golf is the natural venue for business and I started playing golf in order to not be excluded from these events. Unfortunately, I haven't gotten good enough to be taken seriously, except for golf games that involve windmills. Baseball games work well and I also took a customer sailing one time. It's a neutral territory where both parties feel they can relax, let down their barriers and just talk.

—David Brooks, Director of Sales,
Geographic Information Services Inc.

I utilize golf as a primary sporting venue for my company. Golf is a very competitive event, but it also allows the adequate time for developing the basis of the long-term, sustainable relationships. The average game is 4–5 hours, and that allows you to spend quality time with the executive. I am a very competitive person, and it allows me to create the "healthy" competitive environment with my prospect while at the same time determining their respective level of expertise and determining their perspective. Golf is an excellent way of defining the *strategic high ground* with your prospect.

—Kyle Bowker, President and CEO, Nextance Inc.

Do you use sporting events/venues to specifically negotiate deals and/or contracts?

Yes. I have talked numbers, negotiated contracts, and proposed new solutions on the golf course.

—Ben Cronin, Account Executive,
Ceridian Human Resource Solutions

Rarely. I save sports to build relationships and save most of the deal stuff for the office. The relationships provide invaluable information during the contract/sourcing phase of deals. Most times your customer is NOT the person negotiating the contract or the terms.

—Michael S. Macey, Sales Director, Netezza Corporation

I use sporting events as a closing event for new and existing customers. These events are utilized as a *signing ceremony* and as a way of saying *thank you* for their business. I tend not to negotiate the terms of a deal on the golf course, as I leave that process to my sales execution teams. The closing ceremony is more of a venue to show appreciation and gratitude for their confidence in me and my company.

—Kyle Bowker, President and CEO, Nextance Inc.

I leave this up to the client. I have some customers who want to wheel and deal on the course and others who would rather just play the game. Often times, the negotiations are subtle and the opportunities to specifically talk about a deal are narrow. I think you have to take your cue and if you're being given an opportunity to close a deal, then you better take it.

—Daniel M. Jubb, Account Executive,
Hyperion Solutions Corporation

If so, what percentage of contracts negotiated have been made at vendor-sponsored sporting events?

This really varies from client to client. For the most part, I figure less than 50 percent [of deals] are discussed on the course, but that doesn't mean that because the deal wasn't discussed that you haven't made some inroads on the contract. If you and the client don't gel, you may hurt your chances of succeeding in the account. It's important to keep in mind your role as an account executive and not overstep your bounds.

—*Daniel M. Jubb, Account Executive,*
Hyperion Solutions Corporation

30 percent of my signed contracts have at one time been discussed on a golf course.

—*Ben Cronin, Account Executive,*
Ceridian Human Resource Solutions

WHAT DID I DO TO PREPARE?

I started interacting with vendors early on in my career and also served as one during my days in consulting. Today, I've realized that my experience on the sell and execution side of the business equation has been very valuable and has helped me engage with and build better relationships with vendors as a result. In positions where I was managing technology for a business, I actively engaged with vendors to learn more about their products, conduct pilots where appropriate, and implement solutions that were based on third-party products and services to meet the needs of my business customers. One important thing I also did early in my career was to engage with other senior professionals and learn from their strengths with regard to vendor and contract management. I also frequently conducted research on vendor management best practices and put what I read to the test. As I've gone through my career, my network has grown and I've learned a lot watching others on how to use social gatherings and sports as an effective tool for building relationships with vendors in order to get win-win results. Most recently, I've started to expand my vendor practices by implementing several techniques and processes to improve vendor performance. Score carding is one of them.

EXHIBIT 8.2   **Golf and Business on the Links at Pebble Beach, California.**

Source: Used with permission by Ziff Davis Media.

RECOMMENDATIONS

- Simply put—get out and learn the game of golf and get somewhat proficient at it. It is the *de facto sport for business today* and will help build and strengthen your network. If integrated properly with business partners, golf helps establish and build better partnerships, relationships, and trust.

- Conduct vendor quality surveys/ratings for key vendors/partners. Identify areas for improvement and do so in writing in a manner that is consistent across all of your key vendors.

- Take ownership of relationships with key vendors as you climb the IT management ladder. Where applicable, take ownership of the contracts associated with vendors in your domain. Establish solid working relationships with legal council to ensure that IT, legal, and your vendor are on the same page with regard to contract terms and expectations in performance.

- Review your company policies with regard to receiving gifts. Some industries and sectors, like the U.S. Federal Government, have very tight and specific regulations on what their employees can do and receive as a gift. Sporting venue fees or invitations may conflict with policies within some organizations. If you do, however, accept an occasional invitation to play golf or attend a sporting event with a vendor or prospective vendor, know your company rules before you go. I often reciprocate a golf invitation with a vendor and pay for it out of my own pocket. I've also been known to go Dutch on several occasions. Thus, even if you have to foot the bill yourself, sporting events can provide invaluable networking opportunities to say the least and, at best, help establish and possibly improve relationships with your key vendors.

- Professionals wanting to be CIOs today should get some experience on the sell side of the business equation so that they can get experience selling to, servicing, and building relationships with customers and prospects. This can be done via a number of avenues. My preferred option was through IT and business consulting services, since that is exactly what most CIOs are buying today.

ENDNOTES

1. www.famous-quotes-and-quotations.com/albert-einstein-quotes.html (accessed June 3, 2005).
2. "Top 5 ERP Vendors Accounted for 72 Percent of 2004 ERP Revenues, Says AMR Research," Tekrati.com web site, Research News Applications Software (June 15, 2005), www.tekrati.com/T2/Analyst_Research/ResearchAnnouncements Details.asp?Newsid=5311 (accessed July 19, 2005).
3. Ibid.

4. "Favorable Climate for Storage Spending Drives Continued Growth in World-wide Disk Storage Systems Market, IDC Finds," IDC.com web site, press release (June 3, 2005), www.idc.com/getdoc.jsp?containerId=prUS00157505 (accessed July 19, 2005).

5. Ibid.

6. Robert McNeill, "IT Trends: Vendor Management," Forrester Research IDEABYTE (November 25, 2003), www.forrester.com/Research/Print/LegacyIT/0,7208,33200,00.html (accessed July 5, 2005).

7. Ibid.

8. Robert McNeill, and Marc Cecere, "Building the Vendor Management Function," Forrester Research (March 15, 2004), http://www.forrester.com/Research/Document/Excerpt/0,7211,34002,00.html (accessed July 5, 2005).

9. Ibid.

10. David F. Carr, "Corporate Performance Management," *Baseline* magazine (August 13, 2003), www.baselinemag.com/print_article2/0,2533,a=48979,00.asp (accessed July 5, 2005).

11. Ibid.

12. Ibid.

13. Ibid.

14. Eric Berkman, "How to Use the Balanced Scorecard," *CIO* magazine (May 15, 2002), www.cio.com/archive/051502/scorecard.html (accessed July 11, 2005).

15. Paul Arveson, "What Is the Balanced Scorecard?" Balanced Scorecard Institute, 1998, www.balancedscorecard.org/basics/bsc1.html (accessed July 11, 2005).

16. Ibid.

17. Ibid.

18. Berkman, "How to Use the Balanced Scorecard."

19. Ibid.

20. Ibid.

21. Ibid.

22. Ibid.

23. Ibid.

24. Ibid.

25. Ibid.

26. dictionary.reference.com/search?q=outsource (accessed July 30, 2005).

27. Ibid.

28. Jeff Kaplan, "Off-target Offshore Outsourcing?" *Network World* magazine (July 18, 2005), 35, www.networkworld.com, http://www.networkworld.com/columnists/2005/071805kaplan.html (accessed December 10, 2005).

29. Ibid.

30. Editors of *CIO Insight*, "Outsourcing 2003: How Well Are You Managing Your Partners?" *CIO Insight* (November 1, 2003), www.cioinsight.com/print_article2/0,2533,a=112818,00.asp (accessed July 5, 2005).

31. Ibid.

32. Christopher Koch, "A New Game Plan," *CIO* magazine (October 15, 2004), www.cio.com/archive/101504/outsource.html (accessed July 5, 2005).

33. Ibid.

34. Ibid.

35. Susan Cramm, "I.T.: Half-Full," *CIO* magazine (February 1, 2005), www.cio.com/archive/020105/competitive.html (accessed July 5, 2005).

36. Amy Joyce, "Well-Rounded Dealmakers Put Golf on Their Resumes," *Washington Post,* June 13, 2005, D1 and D9.

37. Ibid.

38. Ibid.

39. Ibid.

40. Ibid.

41. Ibid.

42. Ibid.

43. Suzanne Woo, "Women to the Fore," WomenWhoNetwork.com web site, www.womenwhonetwork.com/Articles/golf1.asp (accessed July 5, 2005).

44. Ibid.

45. David James, "Watch That First Step," BSIcorp.net web site, www.bsicorp.net/970421/ (accessed July 5, 2005).

46. Ibid.

47. Harry Hurt III, "How to Play Golf Like a Billionaire," *New York Times,* June 18, 2005, B6.

48. Ibid.

49. Paul Rogers, "Mixing Business & Golf," *BusinessWeek Online/Golf Digest* (November 18, 2002), www.businessweek.com/print/magazine/content/02_46/b3808623.htm (accessed July 5, 2005).

50. Ibid.

51. Thomas Wailgum, "Mastering the Secret Etiquette of Golf," *CIO* magazine (April 1, 2005), www.cio.com/archive/040105/golf.html (accessed May 6, 2005).

CHAPTER 9

Contract Negotiation and Financial Management

Think like a CFO and act like a CIO.

—GREGORY S. SMITH

CONTRACT NEGOTIATION TIPS AND BEST PRACTICES

A CIO, CTO, or other IT executive who doesn't have solid if not *sharpened* contract negotiation skills on top of solid vendor management and relationship skills is not serving his or her organization properly and, simply put, is at risk. As stated previously in this text, the IT department/division is one of the groups in most organizations that manages a large amount of vendors in support of purchased products, services, hosting solutions, and consulting services. That translates to needing solid contract negotiation skills.

Early in my career, I met a young, bright attorney at a Fortune 200 firm that helped show me the light and the importance of having great contract negotiation skills. The firm we represented was in the middle of a dispute with a small but key vendor on whether to pay additional licensing fees to upgrade software that we had previously purchased and whose fees were paid in full on our maintenance agreement. Prior to going live with the software solution, I spent a fair amount of time with my legal counsel, and now my friend, negotiating the business, technical, and legal terms and conditions of the contract. The dispute was simple—the vendor thought that they were entitled to charge us additional fees if we moved beyond our current operating system environment, then Microsoft Windows 95, to Windows NT. We, on the other hand, thought that the language in the contract that dealt with *upgrades and support* was clear and entitled us to code upgrades regardless of the Windows operating system that we were running. After several e-mails and phone calls discussing the issue, we were at a stalemate. The conference call was set for a Thursday afternoon with their CEO and we were ready to do battle.

I started the call and introduced our legal counsel at the onset. We had a brief and polite conversation on the issues—again—and after a relatively short period of time, came to the conclusion that we agreed to disagree. Just when it appeared that the call was going nowhere, my counsel again pointed to the provision in the contract that we interpreted as being entitled to receive free upgrades to the application and that the contract did not specify an operating system at all. Simply put, we were aware that the original contract did not state the supported operating systems and, therefore, that we were entitled to free upgrades on any platform as long as we remained current with our annual maintenance fees. Near the end of the conference call, I politely asked the vendor team for a couple of minutes to discuss some things on our side. I placed them on hold. My legal counsel asked me if we needed to confer or further strategize on our approach. I said no, that I just wanted to allow them two minutes to think about the potential outcomes. We spent the time shooting foam basketballs at the plastic basketball rim mounted on the back of my door. When the call resumed, I made the following statement to their team:

> I've discussed the issue with our legal counsel and you have 48 hours to comply with the terms and conditions in the signed contract or we will sue you for breach of contract with the full legal force of our organization.

After a small and uncomfortable pause, their CEO stated, "We'll have to think about it and get back to you." We didn't hear back from them that day, but the next morning there was a voice mail left for me that simply stated, "The software upgrades are in the mail and you should have them by Monday morning." It was precisely then that I realized the real power of a contract and that proper preparation and contract negotiation were key to IT solutions and deals. I learned several lessons during the negotiation with that vendor that had an impact on me for the rest of my career:

1. Never underestimate a vendor's desire to save money.

2. There are multiple definitions of *customer service*.

3. If key provisions of the deal aren't in writing, the contract isn't worth the paper it's written on.

4. Ambiguity or omission of issues and terms can be a good thing if it can work to your advantage.

5. Negotiate in good faith.

6. Get solid legal counsel involved early in the negotiation process.

The need for contract negotiation skills is high on the list for today's CIOs, but also can include an application dedicated to ensure proper contract management. According to Forrester Research,

> Contract life-cycle management (CLM) applications will experience rapid growth of 40 percent in demand in 2005, driven by the growing desire of enterprises to manage contract creation, negotiation, and compliance on an enterprise-wide basis, to help ensure compliance with Sarbanes-Oxley and to capture savings buried in contracts with suppliers and sales or licensing revenues in contracts with customers or licensees of intellectual property.[1]

In addition, there are a number of mechanisms that organizations and CIOs can take today to reduce the risks associated with weak contracts with vendors and gain control over their domain. Today's IT environments are usually a mix of outsourced and internally managed. Some organizations push the envelope on the outsourced model harder than others. According to a Forrester Research article, General Motors is one company that "has well-honed outsourced management practices."[2] According to the Forrester article, GM has a disciplined contracting process to reduce the number of IT contracts, at one point as high as 600 in number, via the following methods:

- Using global, standardized contracts for IT
- Building in language for pertinent compliance requirements

- Integrating contract review and approval into their central IT governance
- Utilizing *fixed-price* contracts instead of time and materials[3]

In addition, GM uses "service level agreements (SLAs) that are tied to financial consequences," tracks all of its IT projects via a dashboard, scorecards certain vendors each year, and rewards their top vendor performers with an awards ceremony.[4]

SERVICE LEVEL AGREEMENTS

SLAs are an important component to most IT contracts, especially for outsourced or hosted applications. Well-negotiated SLAs include terms for performance across multiple IT domains, including key metrics for network availability, hardware, and application service levels. For hosted solutions, CIOs aim for high-availability guarantees that spell out key issues like (1) uptime percentage minimums, (2) notifications for planned outages, (3) response times for unplanned outages, and (4) penalties for outages that go below contractually agreed-upon minimum thresholds. Best practice IT shops will employ SLAs for their internal staff/systems as well in an effort to better service their internal business customers. According to a recent *eWeek* article and survey of 140 IT professionals that use internal SLAs, failures are leading to more outsourcing.[5] The *eWeek* article goes on to report that for those surveyed, "42 percent of providers are not meeting SLAs 90 percent of the time" and that "outsourcing is a potential outcome for not meeting SLAs."[6]

Metrics for SLAs can be complex, depending on the work and where it is done and should be well thought out before going to the negotiation table. Forrester Research reports that typical service metrics include the following quality indicators: (1) efficiency, (2) effectiveness, (3) quality, (4) timeliness, (5) productivity, and (6) cost.[7] The number of contractually spelled out measurements for these indicators can be lengthy and add to the complexity of the SLA. Examples include uptime, availability, response time, throughput, accuracy, and cost.[8] The Forrester article goes on to suggest three major considerations for SLAs during negotiation:

1. Understand the benefits and impacts of a specific service level.
2. The provider needs to understand the cost of delivering the service level and potential consequences.

3. The provider needs to accurately measure the service level using metrics. If the data aren't properly collected, they can't be measured.[9]

In my experience, through research conducted and in conversations with other seasoned CIOs, I offer the following recommendations with regard to best practices for SLA negotiations, especially for externally hosted or outsourced services:

- Spell out what you want with regard to acceptable planned maintenance windows and notifications prior to conducting the work.

- Spell out clear uptime percentages and specify clear penalties (target fee-based) for failures. A 99.99999% uptime typically means that an unplanned outage is a penalty, whereas a 99.5% uptime allows for approximately 4 hours per month for scheduled maintenance and/or upgrades.

- Request monthly reports for external SLAs to guarantee that the vendor is appropriately collecting the right data and using the defined metrics specified in the contract.

Additional contract provisions beyond SLAs should include:

- Disaster recovery provisions should be stipulated where appropriate and responsibilities spelled out.

- Price is important, but not the only criteria for a good contract. If the vendor isn't making any money, they may not be in business long enough to provide the services that you desire.

- Determine whether you want to go long in duration (and potentially reduce the cost per year) or short on the contract term. I used to go for longer-duration contracts in the past, but have recently switched to shorter-duration terms. It appears that competition for business today by vendors is fierce and that they are willing to give almost identical pricing for shorter-range contract terms as for longer ones.

- Pay attention to annual increases and limits. Negotiate annual caps on the amount or percentage that a vendor can increase their costs for the services provided. An example of a term that I use to collar price creep is to restrict the vendor in any one year from increasing prices beyond the "lesser of x percent or CPI-W," which specifies a floor rate and potentially leverages a declining consumer price index environment as an inflationary hedge.

- Avoid paying annual or full project services up front, especially for large project implementations that involve consulting services and project management resources.

- Tie payments where appropriate to milestones and products delivered.

- Pay attention to penalties for early termination and attempt to reduce or eliminate them.

- Spell out renewal terms. Most vendors love to auto-renew customers if they're not notified within a specific window that is close to the end of the then current term.

- For projects or services that are beyond the IT infrastructure, get your business customers and partners engaged in the contract review and negotiation process. IT should not be the sole negotiator for business unit projects and technical services.

- Where appropriate, properly evaluate internal purchased solutions versus application service provider (ASP) offerings, and do a price comparison to get the best solution. IT shops that are strapped for capital dollars may be best served by looking at ASP offerings and using operating funds.

- Properly evaluate the costs associated with the various licensing options in the contract. Typical options include (1) named users, (2) server-based, (3) central processing unit (CPU)-based, and (4) concurrent users. I personally like named users for smaller licensed applications and concurrent users for larger ones. I avoid CPU-based licensing and feel that it greatly impedes a CIO's ability to grow and scale IT infrastructure to meet performance needs, possibly with the same number of application users.

- Never forget that a contract is one that is *mutually agreed upon* by two or more parties. That said, negotiate the terms and conditions that you really want and need and give on the less important issues.

- Let the lawyers handle the legal sections like force major and indemnification.

- Pay attention to a vendor's right to disclose that your firm is a customer. I typically change this clause to state that I must agree in writing before any disclosure is made and hold that as a performance carrot over their heads. If a vendor performs well and makes a good impression in the first year or so, I'll likely allow them to disclose that my firm is a customer in marketing collateral and may serve as a reference for potential customers. I never serve as a reference after a contract is signed without any indications of performance, regardless of the price and beneficial terms negotiated.

- And finally, pay attention to what you get for *maintenance and upgrades*. Also, pay attention and negotiate down high annual fees and watch out for the percentage that the fee can increase from year to year. Typical annual maintenance fees range from 17 to 20 percent of the purchase price.[10] That's essentially paying the cost of the original system again every 5 years. That said, a well-negotiated maintenance fee could save an organization lots of money in the out years.

I asked a group of CIO experts their feedback on contract negotiation tips. The most common answers are listed below along with a few great comments/recommendations.

CIO SURVEY

List your top five vendor contract negotiation tips.
The most common answers are listed below.

1. Be direct, with open and clear communications.
2. Clarify expectations and deliverables.
3. Be prepared to walk away from a bad contract if necessary.
4. Get legal counsel engaged early and be tough, but fair. You only succeed if your partners/vendors succeed.
5. Do your homework on the options available to you and let the vendor know.

Due to the value of the input, honorable mentions and other frequent comments include the following:

- Identify key resources contractually. These could include project managers and key technical consultants.
- Never be in a hurry.
- Understand the market of the vendor.
- Separate what you must have from the nice to have.
- Determine your needs first, do a request for proposal (RFP) or request for information (RFI) on competing vendors, then begin negotiations.

Additional comments from select CIOs are listed below.

Always understand the material milestones of the salesperson and when the company's quarterly/annual reporting dates are. They will cave if they need to. FYI, I only buy cars between Christmas and New Years and I have always paid under invoice. Be tough but fair and never, ever lie or cheat. Demand the same in return. Eliminate anyone you don't trust (entire vendor or just the sales rep).

—John W. Von Stein, Executive Vice President and CIO,
The Options Clearing Corporation

Try to keep two vendors engaged in legitimate negotiations until the deal is done. In situations where the deal is so big that this is not practical, I tell the second place vendor the truth—that we will come back if #1 can't strike a deal. Do this once and the vendor community will know that you are serious and it will help with future negotiations.

—John R. Sullivan, CIO, AARP

FINANCIAL MANAGEMENT—THINK LIKE A CFO AND ACT LIKE A CIO

Financial management for technology means a lot of different things to different people. One thing is almost assured—CIOs that don't properly manage the financial and budgeting aspects well for their IT shop will likely be reporting to the CFO soon—where proper oversight can be applied. Core financial skills required for today's CIOs include the following:

- Budgeting and planning.

- Knowledge of financial purchasing options—capitalized and depreciated versus operating expenses.

- Basic accounting principles, standards, and understanding the technology impacts and risks associated with implementing cutting edge/new technologies. For example, if you capitalize the purchase of a new technology and take it out of service in the second year, you have write-off issues, since the solution is no longer being depreciated.

- Knowledge of financial models and methods to ensure that IT purchases are worth the investment and match a business need.

- Knowledge of compliance regulations, such as Sarbanes-Oxley, and the impacts to their business including budgeting, expertise, resource planning, reporting, and certification.

What are the most important financial skills that a CIO needs to have today and why?

Budget management, financing and amortization, capital and life cycle planning, and B/C and ROI.

—*David G. Swartz, Vice President and CIO,*
The George Washington University

Management of budget as well as creating ROI on business needs. IT brings about efficiencies in business that should be able to be measured where possible and communicated out to the entire organization.

—*Shyam K. Dunna, CIO/Assistant General Manager, MARTA*
(Metropolitan Atlanta Rapid Transit Authority)

Since IT is one of the biggest investments a firm makes, it is important for the CIO to be able to quantify and qualify its impact, both from a revenue enhancement and cost perspective. A basic understanding of corporate accounting and budgeting practices is inherent in this.

—*Steven W. Agnoli, Chief Information Officer,*
Kirkpatrick & Lockhart Nicholson

Capital Assets

Capital assets are those that typically have a life beyond one year. These include assets such as buildings, furniture, and, yes, computer equipment and systems. CIOs today work closely with finance and accounting staff to ensure that IT assets are accounted for in the proper way. In the United States, companies usually depreciate large or longer-term use IT assets over three to five years, with three years being a typical time for equipment and up to five years for long-term use applications that were purchased and not leased. Thus, the costs of capitalized assets are *depreciated* over a series of years. Assets can be depreciated in equal measures, *straight line,* or via an unequal and *accelerated* manner. This is usually the call of the controller or CFO and something that is usually standardized within most organizations. My experience indicates that the most common method for depreciating IT assets in the United States is straight line. IT equipment purchases such as networking equipment, PC technology refresh, servers, and other IT infrastructure equipment are typically depreciated over three years, while longer-term applications like human resource information systems (HRIS), financial systems, and other enterprise resource planning (ERP) solutions are depreciated for terms closer to five years.

What is the minimum threshold and price for a capital asset? It depends. In the United States, generally accepted accounting principles (GAAP) dictate guidelines for this, but most organizations determine the minimum amount internally. I've seen capital minimums range from a low of $5,000, to a midrange of $50,000, to a high of $100,000. Also, determining which assets to capitalize and depreciate can be tricky. My recommendation: When in doubt, talk to your CFO or controller for guidance.

Operating Expenses

IT products that are expensed are those that typically have a useful life or are consumed in the current fiscal year. In addition to some IT assets and services, staff salary and benefit costs are operating expenses and are typically included as part of the overall IT operating budget. Examples of IT assets that are commonly expensed include, but are not limited to, (1) training, (2) software/hardware maintenance fees, (3) software upgrade fees, (4) IT publications/books purchased, (5) travel, (6) transaction-oriented fees associated with ASPs, (7) telecommunications fees, (8) application/server hosting fees, and (9) Internet bandwidth fees. Some organizations expense desktop and laptop computers, especially if purchased in small quantities where they may fall below the organization's minimum capital threshold. However, others that purchase these assets in bulk and exceed an organization's minimum capital threshold capitalize the asset since it typically has a useful life of 3 or more years.

Most organizations today utilize a mix of capital and operating expense approaches for purchasing IT assets and systems in an effort to *equitably distribute the cost of the expected useful life of the asset.* The impact on an organization's financial books for capitalized IT assets is essentially one that could yield a more positive outcome on earnings before income tax (EBIT) since the costs associated with the purchase are spread out over several years and don't all hit in the current fiscal year. In contrast, the impact of IT assets that are expensed on EBIT could mean lower net income (if profitable) and thus a lower tax liability. Organizations can get into trouble if they select the wrong method. Recent bankruptcies in the United States brought on the need for additional government Securities Exchange Commission (SEC) regulations to mitigate this risk. Auditors today are on the lookout to ensure that IT assets or systems purchased are properly accounted for. An example of an auditing red flag may include an IT asset that should have been expensed in the current year, but was capitalized in an effort to spread the cost over multiple years in an effort to improve the financial net income of the firm for the current year. When in doubt, you should engage your financial specialists and, if necessary, ask your auditor.

Financial Models—Return on Investment

Financial models are an interesting issue for CIOs. Some use and rely heavily on analysis and outcome, while others avoid them like the plague and think that they're best suited for the *pure* financial specialists or business counterparts in their organization. The most common financial model used by CIOs today is return on investment (ROI). ROI is an easy calculation and is defined by most financial professionals as "the amount of earnings taken in divided by the amount invested to generate the earnings."[11] Unfortunately, the calculation for the ROI associated with IT investments isn't that easy to calculate and measure.

ROI analyses can be conducted before and after a project is selected and implemented. According to a recent *CIO Insight* article reporting results for 370 IT executives surveyed, 84 percent use ROI for initial project justification and 46 percent use it for completed projects.[12] In addition, the *CIO Insight* article indicated that only 17 percent of CIO respondents stated that they generally trusted ROI information from vendors, while 68 percent stated that using ROIs have had a positive impact on aligning IT to the business.[13] Vendors have been quick to embrace the ROI bandwagon as well, often touting the financial advantages of their offerings to prospective customers via presentations and online calculators. According to *CIO* magazine, "the problem with these [vendor] ROI calculators is that they are focused only on the financial factor."[14] The *CIO* magazine article goes on to suggest that IT executives today should look beyond ROI and for a *return on value* (ROV), which goes beyond just financial aspects and takes into consideration other tangible and intangible issues like competition, culture, strategic alignment, business, and technical value.[15]

Pressure for CIOs to use some kind of model to help justify IT investment is on the rise, especially if they've not yet proven themselves to other business executives. According to a *CIO Insight* article and survey of 404 IT executives, 60 percent say "the pressure to calculate ROI is on the rise," while only 2 percent feel that the need is decreasing.[16] There are several ROI methods, but "cost reduction is the most commonly used ROI method at 77 percent, followed by customer satisfaction at 57 percent and productivity improvement at 56 percent."[17] There are also several flavors of ROI used today. *Average ROI* "indicates the gains that a group of companies reported after deploying a given technology."[18] As this method goes, if a group of customers are satisfied with a technology or product, then the average ROI is high. *Cumulative ROI* "sums the gains made by a specific company over a certain length of time."[19] According to a *CIO* magazine article, this method can be extremely flawed since it aggregates returns in an unreasonable fashion and gives the perception that there are more returns than there really are.[20] The article goes on to suggest that cumulative ROI is misleading "of what will happen in the crucial first year, and of the likely payback."[21]

The best and most accurate ROI method used is *annual ROI* (aROI), which measures returns in each year, relative to the initial IT investment.[22] I often look at a ROI, but also perform a *break-even* calculation on an IT investment where appropriate to get a more accurate return estimate. For example, when calculating the break-even for an investment in Internet protocol (IP) phones, I looked at the initial cost of the hardware, installation, training, and service fees and then calculated the break-even period based on an estimated savings for reduced toll calls. The estimate for the toll calls was not a guesstimate and was based on a detailed analysis of call volume and bills for a variety of locations that I was considering for the IP phones. Thus, when combined with a break-even analysis, an annual ROI can be an effective tool.

Other Models

Other models and tools used by CIOs and IT professionals today to help justify IT investments include total cost of ownership (TCO), net present value (NPV), and internal rate of return (IRR). TCO attempts to identify the lifetime cost of a particular asset, which typically goes out several years past the initial purchase date and price. The classic TCO war and analysis in the past was to compare the total cost of ownership of the standard personal computer (PC) versus the networked computer (NC). Analysts crunched the numbers six ways to Sunday in an effort to show that the lifetime costs associated with purchasing, training for, and maintaining an NC were lower than those for a PC. To make a long story short, the TCO for an NC was probably lower than that of a PC, but it failed to convince buyers to abandon their beloved decentralized and *fat client* computing device. In the end, the NC failed and the PC lives on.

NPV and IRR measure more than a traditional ROI since they take into consideration the expected life of an investment, including depreciation and the cost of capital. These models are often used at mature capital-intensive companies.[23] CIOs are sometimes tempted to use vendor-created models, and anything else they can get their hands on, to show that they're not just spending money on IT without a positive financial analysis or a real business benefit. I never take a vendor ROI at face value and believe that CIOs need to work with their business counterparts to identify benefits that can be derived from a typical IT investment intended to benefit the organization. Unfortunately, there is no exact science or a one-model-fits-all approach. Today's CIOs must be creative and go beyond just models. Simply put, some things can't be justified through a financial cost benefit or model. Today's IT environment is a world where IT systems and the results that show up are unstructured and intangible. This intangible or hard-to-quantify aspect of IT makes it difficult to measure and build into an accurate model. Some things such as productivity and impact on customer service are hard to measure with certain IT investments. So, what's a CIO to do? Use models where they make sense and can easily be defined and measured against results. Where they don't work well, don't use them. Forced ROI analysis from CFOs or other executives may be a bigger symptom of a lack of trust. Once a track record of on-time and on-budget deliverables is established, many CIOs can simply cruise through a part of their annual budgeting process, typically infrastructure, without having to do any ROI or analysis.

The Power of Compliance

Regulations and laws are a powerful way to enforce change. CIOs today, especially ones that work in public for-profit organizations, must be acutely aware of laws that impact the IT organization and chart a course to be compliant with those laws. In the United States, the most important new legislation was the passage of the Sarbanes-Oxley Act of 2002. Section 404 of Sarbanes-Oxley requires CEOs and CFOs to certify that they have sufficient internal controls over financial reporting and that they must be met annually. Since most organizations use financial systems and applications to manage their books, many of the business processes that demonstrate SOA compliance are supported by technology—thus the engagement of the CIO. According to a *CIO* magazine CIO Executive Council poll of 162 members, 70 percent of the respondents indicated that the responsibility for Sarbanes-Oxley compliance was as a *team* effort, headed by the CFO, CIO, and supporting staff.[24] In addition, the CIO Executive Council poll found that 73 percent understood the SOA requirements, 49 percent didn't think they were fair, 82 percent indicated that their organizations were pressing ahead with a 100 percent commitment, and 11 percent indicated that they would just do enough to get by.[25] According to a February 2005 *CIO* magazine article, the following recommendations were offered up for existing and new CIOs dealing with Sarbanes-Oxley:

- *Bring in business sponsors.* IT should work alongside finance and accounting staff to refine controls, both process oriented and technically preventative.
- *Overestimate your costs from the beginning.*
- *Put the best people on the job.* This includes IT, internal audit, and finance and accounting staff.
- *Visualize it.* Use visual and graphic aids to document process flows and controls.

After the audit, it's not business as usual.[26]

The auditing and professional services costs associated with Sarbanes-Oxley for public companies has been increasing since the day the Act was signed in 2002. According to officials at PricewaterhouseCoopers LLP, one of the largest accounting firms, "the law has resulted in profound changes in behavior," and folks at Deloitte & Touche LLP indicated that approximately 140 companies were found to have insufficient controls and weaknesses as of March 30, 2005.[27] Regulators initially thought that complying with Sarbanes-Oxley internal controls would cost a publicly traded company about $91,000, but according to a study by Financial Executives International, the costs have increased to approximately $4.3 million per company and the largest ones are paying even more.[28] During a recent presentation that I sat in on, the CEO of a public technology powerhouse company indicated that they estimated their auditing fees would double between the first year of compliance with Sarbanes-Oxley and the prior year of noncompliance. They were wrong. Their costs increased fourfold and were close to $10 million in the first year of compliance. Some folks are flat out angry at the increased costs, time, and ambiguity of the language in section 404. According to the finance chief at Urban Outfitters, "Senators Sarbanes and Oxley should have to spend a month in any company trying to comply with the unclear and monotonous requirements being imposed by the Big Four auditors."[29] Implications of Sarbanes-Oxley go beyond just financial costs. According to a *Washington Post* article, between 2003 and 2004—just three years after the passage of Sarbanes-Oxley—audit fees for Fortune 1000 companies have increased 63 percent, CFO turnover at Fortune 500 companies is up 23 percent, and annual financial restatements are up 28 percent.[30] According to *CIO Insight*, in August 2005, the Public Company Accounting Oversight Board (PCAOB) and the SEC "attempted to clear up two of the most costly vagaries of the Sarbanes-Oxley Act," by releasing new guidance for defining *material weakness*.[31] According to the *CIO Insight* article, Paul Hamerman, vice president of enterprise applications at Forrester Research, "thinks that the moves by the two governing bodies will help in clarifying SarbOx compliance," but concedes that the "language is less than direct" and that "it's possible a CIO might not get it."[32]

Based on the amount of money and time organizations are investing to become certified with Sarbanes-Oxley, it quickly rises high on the list of financial management tasks for CIOs today. Even nonprofit CIOs are starting to take Sarbanes-Oxley seriously. I personally believe that it's just a matter of time for a derivative or subset of Sarbanes-Oxley to hit the nonprofit sector. Thus, most proactive nonprofit CIOs have already started getting their IT house in order. That includes paying more attention to security and access controls for financial systems, asset tracking, change management, and best practice IT governance.

BUDGETING AND FORECASTING—
ALIGNING IT WITH BUSINESS STRATEGY

How important is it for CIOs today to have solid budgeting and forecasting skills? In short—very important. The first question that I was asked during the interview process for my first CIO appointment was, "What was the largest budget you've managed in your career to date?" The second question was, "Give me an example of a successful cost reduction you led." I responded with the size of the largest budget I was accountable for and indicated that I had successfully saved a prior organization $12.5 million by reversing a fully outsourced ERP application support contract with a mix of internal staff and reduced consulting support. That said, the following guidelines are designed to help CIOs and subordinates get a better handle on their IT budgets:

- *Don't guess at the costs.* Get a handle on the business requirements first, before researching possible solutions. Low guesses that are approved for funding that are exceeded during implementation won't get any confidence points from the CFO or your boss.

- *Know what IT purchases are capital expenditures and which ones are operating expenses and budget accordingly.* Most large projects involve some capital and operating expenses. Make sure that you capture all of the right components such as training, hardware maintenance, software maintenance, implement/project management fees, transaction fees, licensing costs, and hosting fees (if applicable).

- *Budget in detail.* I like to budget at the line item level for most large projects and require my subordinates to do the same for their budgets that roll up to my accountability. That said, an entry of $100,000 for training doesn't cut it in my book. I like to see the line item support to justify *all of the training* components that will make up the full $100,000. The devil is in not showing the details.

- *Use a consistent model or system for budgeting.* Smaller firms may opt for a Microsoft Excel–based solution, while larger firms typically utilize an enterprise budgeting system. There are several vendors on the market to handle some very complex enterprise budgeting requirements. Do your research before you buy.

- *Facilitate business buy-in where appropriate.* For projects that involve the business staff, use methodologies to justify the benefit to the organization, specify metrics for success, and get their buy-in and ownership before going to the mat for them during budget defense.

- *Learn how to adjust and reforecast quickly.* If you've gone over in a project that could have a material impact on your budget for the year, don't wait to engage your supervisor or the CFO. If you're under budget, consider giving some money back to other parts of the organization instead of simply spending the excess on IT. I love to compare my IT budgets to industry benchmarks and personally strive to come in below the industry average. A benchmark that I use is to compare my IT budget (including staff, capital, and operating expenses) as a percentage of overall revenue and benchmark the results against other best practice firms and industry research and trends.

- *Pay attention to contracts and maintenance fee increases.* Failure to build in contractually agreed-upon maximum increases for maintenance and support for multiyear agreements/systems can impact your budget in a negative way if not properly accounted for in your estimate.

- *Be honest on the impacts of deep cuts.* I typically run the numbers for multiple budgeting scenarios that include (1) keeping the lights on, (2) including only critical enhancements and revenue-generating projects, and (3) nice-to-have projects. If you're asked to go below keeping the base core IT infrastructure and key business applications running, be prepared to cut some services or sunset applications/systems that aren't delivering value to the organization anymore. Savvy CIOs view budget defense as an artful negotiation.

In today's budget-aware IT environment, CIOs that don't proactively manage their IT budgets will likely be reporting to someone who will and who most likely will also have final signatory for large IT purchases. I asked my CIO group their thoughts on the importance of budgeting and planning experience for today's CIO appointments.

How important is budgeting experience and budget size managed in landing a *first-time* CIO appointment?

- 53 percent responded with *high.*
- 29 percent responded with *medium.*
- 6 percent responded with *low.*
- 12 percent did not respond.

This is the language of the business. If you cannot master this, you will be destined to live with what you get rather than leading the discussion of how the organization should use its resources.

—Hans Keller, Chief Technology Officer,
National Aquarium in Baltimore

TOOLS TO MINIMIZE FINANCIAL RISK

There are a number of ways that IT professionals and CIOs can reduce risk associated with an IT investment. I asked a group of world-class CIOs their thoughts.

What financial tools (if any), do you use to ensure that IT is delivering value for the investment?

The most common answers given include:

- ROI calculations
- Budget tracking tools
- Revenue creation report
- Monthly financial reports and variances

Several. They include a profit and loss statement for IT, a balance sheet for IT, IT spending as a percentage of revenue, and ROI on key initiatives.

—Mykolas Rambus, CIO, W.P. Carey.

Additional mechanisms that CIOs use today to minimize and reduce the risk associated with IT purchases include

- using ASPs and outsourcing to reduce capital purchases and offset a possible lack of internal IT skills and staff to properly manage an implemented system.

- using financial models where appropriate and expected by other executives in the organization.

- using consistent methodologies to properly document business justifications and needs and to better estimate costs.

- utilizing project management tools and approaches. Portfolio management of IT and business unit projects can help CIOs see the big picture of where their budget is at any point in the year. Portfolio management is intended to augment financial reports, not replace them.

- where appropriate, using RFPs and RFIs to get estimates from consulting firms regarding defined requirements, implementation costs, and realistic timing estimates.

- conducting technology pilots where available. A lot of information can be gained by rolling out a particular solution to a group of users instead of the entire staff. Build in pilots to contracts and define the scope and duration with vendors where appropriate. I've found that most vendors are willing to risk an organization test driving their technology at a fixed or free pilot cost. I typically build terms and conditions for the pilot and acceptance directly into the contract. If the pilot succeeds, the contract is live. If it fails, the contract is terminated.

- using SLAs to get better performance from vendors, minimize support headaches, and spell out penalties and payments from the vendor if they miss their targets.

- getting buy-in from business unit executives for their projects that have an IT impact.

MAKING FRIENDS WITH THE CFO

Seasoned CIOs and midlevel IT rising stars should never lose sight of trying to make friends and even impress the CFO with their financial acumen and skills. Typically, CFOs are the worst nightmare for a CIO, since they usually have a significant say in how an organization spends money from year to year. According to a *CIO* magazine article, "CFOs always look at [a proposal] and say, What's my return on investment?"[33] Typical CIO responses to justify the spending include nonfinancial benefits like additional functionality, productivity enhancements, or simply needed infrastructure upgrades. Either way, the CIO and CFO usually are speaking different languages and approaching purchases from different perspectives. Is it easier for a CFO to learn the ins and outs of technology to help justify IT purchases or for CIOs to learn the *financial lingo* and start thinking like a CFO when it comes to budgeting and spending money on IT projects? I firmly believe in the latter. The following tips can help CIOs and IT line managers with budget and signatory responsibility better communicate IT spending to their CFO:

- *Tie spending to a business owner.* It helps to have a solid business case, metrics for success, and a business owner that is willing to help push the initiative.

- *Speak in financial terms.* When speaking with CFOs, speak their language. Be prepared to discuss any financial models used to justify the spending as well as soft benefits to the organization if hard to quantify with a financial model.

- *Come to the table with multiple options.* When justifying a major IT/business purchase, a CIO should be prepared to discuss the anticipated costs, initial and out years, as well as the pros and cons to purchase options. These can include, but are not limited to (1) purchased and implemented internally, (2) partially outsourced and run internally, (3) fully outsourced, or (4) run through an ASP. These options have varying impacts on the purchasing strategy. For example, if an organization has more operating dollars than capital, then an ASP or outsourced solution may be a better recommendation to the CFO.

- *Make a recommendation.*[34] After the business need is discussed and the financial purchasing options fully vetted, make your recommendation with confidence. A prepared and financially grounded CIO is one that can wield money like a sword.

WHAT DID I DO TO PREPARE?

As early as possible in my career, I volunteered to take on vendor management, contract management, and budgeting responsibilities for key systems and solutions within my IT domain. I also partnered with legal counsel to learn the ins and outs of contract negotiation and the language used within agreements. Proficiency to me was taking a draft addendum to legal counsel, only to have minor corrections, usually in the areas of the law and not in IT or business terms. I also leveraged mentors and experts within and outside the various organizations where I worked for advice on best practice budgeting and forecasting techniques. I'm the kind of person who doesn't like to reinvent the wheel on something that is done in every organization on the planet—like contract negotiation and budgeting. I also learned the accuracy advantages of budgeting at a line item level versus a more general approach at a Fortune 200 financial services firm. In order to get more accurate budgetary numbers, I research solutions, conduct interviews with key vendors, and utilize RFPs and RFIs to get more accurate numbers. In short, spending time on the budgeting and planning portion of IT should get more accurate numbers for which to set a trend going forward and help in the defense of your budget. In my graduate business program, I learned and soon applied the finance and accounting fundamentals and models that CFOs and other financial professionals use in their discipline. It was in my graduate business program that I really learned the value of speaking the CFO's language in both planning and looking at creating financial options for payment.

RECOMMENDATIONS

This chapter to me was an important one to write in this text and one that I could have probably spent an entire book describing. I can't stress enough the need for today's and tomorrow's CIOs to be financially grounded and savvy in contract management, negotiation, budgeting, and use of models. Below are some recommendations to get up to speed:

- Get some financial expertise and take ownership (preferably through signatory) over your IT budget.
- Get experience managing and negotiating contracts. Find a legal mentor to help you through the process.

- Get experience in managing vendor relationships. Contract and negotiation ownership usually comes with owning the relationship.

- Use methodologies and project management best practices to control cost and project scope creep.

- Get up to speed on financial models and purchase options. Where appropriate, engage finance and accounting professionals for advice and guidance. Get business units involved in ROI and ROV analysis. Use methodologies to document value to the business and define the metrics to measure before considering going down an ROI path. Evaluate model options carefully before jumping in and know the pros and cons of each. Ask your CFO what he or she wants to see with regard to justifying IT investments.

- Get an MBA or tech-MBA. I've said this numerous times in this text and so have the CIOs and executive recruiters that I've interviewed.

- Get business unit buy-in and ownership for non-IT infrastructure projects.

- Find a mentor to help build your contract negotiation and financial skills.

- Research best practices for RFPs and RFIs in an effort to save time and money. There is a lot of useful information available from both paid IT advisory firms as well as free publicly available information on proposal best practices. Use templates where appropriate to standardize processes and documents.

ENDNOTES

1. Andrew Bartels, John Ragsdale, Connie Moore, and Natalie Lambert, "Trends 2005: Contract Life-Cycle Management" (Cambridge, MA: Forrester Research), November 9, 2004, www.forrester.com/Research/Print/Document/0,7211,35693,00.html (accessed August 1, 2005).

2. Laurie M. Orlov, Julie Giera, Robert McNeill, and Christine Ferrusi Ross, "GM's Well-Honed Outsourcer Management Practices" (Cambridge, MA: Forrester Research), June 6, 2005, www.forrester.com/Research/Print/Document/0,7211,37079,00.html (accessed August 1, 2005).

3. Ibid.

4. Ibid.

5. Paula Musich, "Report: SLA Failures Boost Outsourcing," *eWeek* (September 5, 2005), 20.

6. Ibid.

7. Jean-Pierre Garbani, Bob Zimmerman, and Stephan Wenninger, "Best Practices for Service-Level Management" (Cambridge, MA: Forrester Research), December 1, 2004, www.forrester.com/Research/Print/Document/0,7211,34894,00 .html (accessed August 1, 2005).

8. Ibid.

9. Ibid.

10. Ben Worthen, "No Tolerance for High Maintenance," *CIO* magazine (June 1, 2003), www.cio.com/archive/060103/vendor.html (accessed August 9, 2005).

11. Ian Springsteel, "Money Talk," *CIO* magazine (January 1, 2001), www.cio.com/ archive/010101/money.html (accessed September 16, 2005).

12. Editors of *CIO Insight,* "ROI 2004: How Well Do You Work with the Business?" *CIO Insight,* April 1, 2004, www.cioinsight.com/print article2/ 0,1217,a=124744,00.asp (accessed September 9, 2005).

13. Ibid.

14. Maria DeGiglio (Robert Frances Group), "Finding Real ROI," *CIO* magazine, 2001, www2.cio.com/analyst/report278.html (accessed September 16, 2005).

15. Ibid.

16. Terry A. Kirkpatrick (Microsoft Watch), "ROI 2002: How Do CIOs Figure ROI?" *CIO Insight,* March 18, 2002, www.cioinsight.com/print_article2/ 0,1217,a=24208,00.asp (accessed September 9, 2005).

17. Ibid.

18. Rebecca Wetteman, "Lies, Damn Lies and Average ROI," *CIO* magazine, October 15, 2003, www.cio.com/archive/101503/work.html (accessed September 16, 2005).

19. Ibid.

20. Ibid.

21. Ibid.

22. Ibid.

23. Springsteel, "Money Talk."

24. Carrie Matthews, "How to Prepare for Sox Compliance," *CIO* magazine (February 1, 2005), 69.

25. Ibid, 70.

26. Ibid.

27. Carrie Johnson, "Public Companies Complain to SEC About Audit Costs," *Washington Post,* April 9, 2005, E1.

28. Ibid., E2.

29. Ibid.

30. Carrie Johnson, "Higher Audit Fees, More Accountability. Sarbanes-Oxley, Three Years Later," *Washington Post,* July 30, 2005, D1.

31. Debra D'Agostino, "SarbOX Guidance Clears Up Nothing," *CIO Insight* (June 5, 2005), www.cioinsight.com/article2/0,1397,1828548,00.asp (accessed June 30, 2005).

32. Ibid.

33. Derek Slater, "Getting in Touch With Your Inner CFO," *CIO* magazine (June 15, 2002), www.cio.com/archive/071502/cfo.html (accessed September 16, 2005).

34. Ibid.

CHAPTER 10

Risk/Reward and Knowing When to Jump

Only those who will risk going too far can possibly find out how far one can go.

—T.S. Elliot[1]

RISK AND REWARD—NOTHING WAGERED, NOTHING GAINED

Taking risks is part of any executive level job. In technology, it's almost a given that CIOs will take risk in order to meet or exceed the goals and drivers pushing the business forward. Given that technology changes so quickly, it is almost impossible for today's technology leaders to take no risk at all—even if their organization is risk averse and their strategies match that profile. Also, today's commodity-driven and decentralized computing environment by nature introduces far more risk than the days when mainframe computing was the norm. Yes, the personal computer and the Internet have changed everything. Balancing technology change with aggressive and changing business drivers is what CIOs are tasked with today, and it is called risk management.

Enterprise risk management is "the integrated management of business risk, financial risk, operational risk and risk transfer to maximize a firm's

shareholder value" according to a recent *CIO* magazine article.[2] A simplified definition might read like: "Risk is knowing the probability and then
managing with that imperfect information."[3] The *CIO* magazine article
goes on to recommend the following three steps to risk assessment (see
Exhibit 10.1):

1. Identify risks, breaking them into internal and external categories
   by risk type

2. Prioritize risks from high to low along with the likelihood of
   impact

3. Strategize to minimize the risk via one of several models[4]

The strategy used most often depends on the risk, but the *CIO* magazine article recommends one of four viable options: (1) avoidance, (2) mitigation, (3) acceptance, or (4) transfer.[5] The *avoidance* approach would
simply prevent the situation that creates the risk in the first place. Example:
Don't change the business logic for how we renew customers.[6] *Mitigating* a
risk involves taking steps to minimize or remove a specific risk entirely.[7]

EXHIBIT IO.I   RISK ASSESSMENT (IDENTIFY RISKS)

Risk Types	Internal	External
Political	Personal agendas cause delays	Regulations affect growth
Cultural	Access to data is threat to fiefdoms	Customers dislike new system
Economic	Accounting changes affect financials	Recession impacts donations
Environmental	Office relocation impacts data access	Unstable power threatens BCP
Technical		
Continuity	Viruses cause downtime	ERP processing errors cause delays
Data integrity	Dirty data delay system migration	New system doesn't match requirements
Change management	Users don't accept new ERP system	Training new users impacts staff time

Source: Used with permission and adapted from "Risks Rewards," *CIO* magazine, November 1, 2004.

Acceptance is a strategy that I would consider to be more risk aware. It acknowledges a risk, but presses ahead anyway. An example might be installing a new human resource information system (HRIS) with not enough HR staff trained or appropriate buy-in from the business unit. The *transfer* approach mitigates a particular risk by moving it to another party, say external, or hedging against it in another way.[8] An example might be to put additional insurance on the IT infrastructure to hedge damage from a flood or fire for assets that may require additional consulting costs and assistance to re-install.

Technology risk management is not a new strategy today, but one that just has more exposure and awareness due to other public events and drivers. Some recent examples of such drivers include (1) the September 11, 2001, attacks on the United States and the risks found by companies greatly affected; (2) increased security threats associated with complexities and increasing attacks of viruses, worms, and spyware; (3) public exposure to corporate and personal data theft and security breaches; (4) corporate fraud cases such as those involving Enron, MCI, and Adelphia; (5) and recent legislation like the Sarbanes-Oxley Act of 2002 (see Exhibit 10.2).

The benefits of establishing and practicing risk management are clear: proactively managing and making better decisions with more information

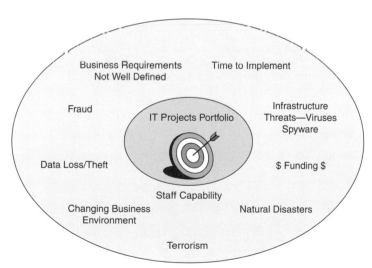

EXHIBIT 10.2   **Risk Drivers Impacting IT Projects and Strategies**

on risks, driving better operational efficiencies, and minimizing financial exposure and impact. There are also some hidden benefits associated with risk management. Selling projects at budget time based on risk may also be easier than trying to quantify them by other methods. Many CIOs that didn't have ample budgets for best practice disaster recovery and business continuity had a much easier sell to increase their budgets and improve their disaster recovery plans after the September 11 attacks in the United States. Also, risks identified by external sources such as auditors and consulting partners can sometimes help sell a change in strategy by pointing out risk from an independent party. Legislation also tends to be a no-brainer driver to mitigate risk due to the penalties for noncompliance. Recent examples include the Health Insurance Portability and Accountability Act of 1996 (HIPPA) and Sarbanes-Oxley.

I asked my group of CIOs their thoughts on risk. Their answers are below and consistent with my expectations.

CIO SURVEY

What is your risk profile and why?

- 24 percent responded with *high.*
- 11 percent responded with between *medium and high.*
- 53 percent responded with *medium.*
- 6 percent responded with *low.*
- 6 percent did not respond.

An additional comment from a select member is listed below.

If you are unwilling to take risks, then you will never achieve any dramatic improvements for your company or your career. If you take too many risks, sooner or later you are going to find yourself on the outside looking in. The idea is to become expert at risk management (trust your gut).

—Carol F. Knouse, Senior Vice President
and CIO, The Donna Karan Company LLC

Can a CIO be successful today without taking risks? If so, why?

- 65 percent responded with *no.*
- 6 percent responded with *yes.*

- 18 percent responded with *other comments.*
- 11 percent did not respond.

Some additional comments from select members are listed below.

Risks are part of the game. Change always comes with risks. But the key is to manage the risks and understand that a CIO only gets so many strikes or failures. But you often have to make mistakes to learn. Just let the other folks make the mistakes and you learn from that.

—David G. Swartz, Vice President and CIO,
The George Washington University

Only in places where legacy is acceptable. It also depends on your definition of "successful."

—Earl Monsour, Director, Strategic Information Technologies,
Maricopa Community College District

Not as a CIO . . . as Director of IT maybe.

—Gerald McCartney, Assistant Dean and CIO,
Krannert School of Management, Purdue University

HOW TO MITIGATE RISKS AND STILL SUCCEED

CIOs can't eliminate risk today, but they can take steps to mitigate risk for projects, IT strategies, and system implementations. Throughout my career, I'm proud to say that I've consistently taken *calculated risks* with a variety of new technologies, enterprise resource planning (ERP) implementations and upgrades, wireless and satellite technologies, and even software development. That said, I attempt to follow best practice and common sense guidelines for risk management by identifying key risks, prioritizing them (sorted by worst case to best case impact), and attempting to eliminate or minimize the risks via *avoidance, mitigation,* and *transfer* strategies. If a project is in the early stages with vendors involved, migrating some of the risks to a vendor/partner may be a good opportunity. That's where the value of good contract negotiation and a sound vendor management strategy becomes really important. Below are some additional techniques used by some of today's leading CIOs.

CIO SURVEY

What steps do you take to mitigate taking known risks?
The best and most common responses are listed below:

- Conduct third-party assessments.
- Do a return on investment (ROI) or other financial analysis before pushing for funding and implementing.
- Get business unit (at the vice president level or higher) buy-in for projects that drive revenue, involve customer support, and are owned by the business.
- Conduct IT advisory research on vendor products and solutions.
- Solicit feedback from peers and staff for similar system implementations.
- Create a contingency plan.
- Thoroughly understand what you are trying to achieve. I'd take this further by recommending a business case justification and full-blown requirements analysis that is signed off by the business unit.
- Identify any risks and critical paths for success. Develop a threat matrix and manage risk throughout the project.
- Put the right project manager on the job and, if possible, have that person reside in the business unit for ownership purposes.
- Don't re-invent the wheel—utilize experienced vendors and consultants where appropriate.
- Build a good team for critical projects that work well together, are motivated, and are in pursuit of a common goal.

In addition to the comments from the CIO group, I've also used the following techniques to minimize risk in my career:

- Conduct technology pilots where appropriate. Before fully deploying a new or risky solution to a large number of users, try out the technology via a smaller pilot group of users. I've done this successfully on a number of projects, including (1) anti-SPAM, (2) remote access software, (3) satellite technology (fixed and mobile), (4) antivirus, (5) software distribution, (6) business intelligence, and (7) wireless personal digital assistants (PDAs). Where possible, you should build in the trial period to your contract with the vendor and attempt to negotiate a free or low-cost trial period. If the product or service is solid, the vendor should have no problem with this approach. Beware of the vendors that won't bite on a limited trial.

- Spend time negotiating favorable terms and conditions and service level agreements for contracts. I can't say enough about this recommendation.

- Use methodologies and sound project management techniques to get to accurate requirements for a sound business need. Conduct research, perform due diligence on vendors and products, get legal counsel involved for contracts, and use peer networking where appropriate to gain insights from others on best practices and lessons learned for similar implementations.

COMMON MISTAKES MADE

CIOs today can make many mistakes as part of managing and mitigating risk. While some failures in IT occur because of pushing out immature technology, systems, and solutions that may not be fully tested, others can fail by simply not acting fast enough. Holding onto legacy technology or systems beyond their useful life is an example of what not to do. According to a recent *CIO* magazine article, "the crash of a critical legacy system at Comair is a classic risk management mistake that cost the airline $20 million and badly damaged its reputation."[9] The article goes on to describe a series of events and decisions that led the airline to postpone for several years the replacement of their sorely aging system, put in place in 1986, to manage flight crews.[10] Distractions included a lack of confidence in the vendor's replacement Windows-based system, managing Y2K, the purchase of the carrier by Delta in 2000, a pilot strike in 2001, and finally the September 11 attacks.[11] As the story goes, a replacement system was approved in 2004, but the cutover to the new system didn't happen soon enough. "The legacy system failed, bringing down the entire airline, canceling or delaying 3,900 flights, and stranding nearly 200,000 passengers."[12] Managing risks associated with older/legacy systems can be tricky, especially when the cost to replace them can easily outpace the original cost, sometimes by magnitudes. Examples of indicators and triggers that CIOs use to determine the right *time* to replace legacy systems today include the following:

- When the vendor that developed and/or supports the legacy system is no longer reliable or in business. If a vendor becomes unreliable and the business experiences significant impacts, the business units will turn on you to quickly map a strategy to improve the situation. All CIOs know that business customers don't care how things get solved—but that they do get solved. That said, managing a key IT vendor is a key part of risk management that needs special attention, especially during system crises.

- When your staff and consulting support can no longer maintain the application either due to aging technology or a skill set gap with technology that is commonly used and found in the IT market-place. Once the resources become scarce to maintain the application (even at a high cost), it's time to aggressively start looking at alternatives.

- When you've had repeated system outages that impact the business in a negative way. Examples include, but are not limited to, (1) lack of system availability during normal business hours or peak times, (2) reduced or diminished customer service, (3) financial loss, and (4) damage to the business brand or reputation.

Additional mechanisms to hedge risks associated with legacy systems include the following:

- Building a contingency plan that includes staff and consultants to provide ongoing support for upgrades and enhancements. Make sure that your staff and consulting support know how to maintain the application. If the skill set isn't there, get it there quickly or start looking at a replacement system that is more easily maintained and supported with skill sets readily available in the IT marketplace.

- Keeping documentation up to date for changes and operational procedures. A classic sign of an aging system is one that is hard to maintain and has little or no documentation. If you're in this boat, start looking at the requirements for a new solution and chart a course for a reliable replacement.

- Ensuring that backup and recovery procedures are tested and working. A sure-fire way for a CIO to get fired is via the loss of critical data, especially for mission-critical systems that support and drive the business.

I asked a group of CIO experts their thoughts on risk and how much they've taken in their careers. The more creative answers are provided below.

For me, a risk that I would have preferred to avoid was selecting a large business intelligence software provider, at the start of some minor financial problems, in support of a major business intelligence and analysis implementation project for an organization where I worked. Shortly after selecting the vendor, signing the contract, and starting implementation, the vendor reported significant financial problems that set off a chain reaction for other negative activities that included damage to their brand, loss of customers, a Securities Exchange Commission (SEC) investigation, a company downsize, and a retrenchment strategy change and focus. In light of the risks, their product was excellent, so I decided to weather the storm. That storm lasted far longer than I'd hoped—multiple years—but the firm and their products recovered back to a state of reliability and financial creditworthiness. My risk management strategy for this issue was one of *acceptance* and one that I don't often use. I guess the outcome could have been far worse, but for me the situation still wasn't an optimal one.

CIO SURVEY

What is the biggest risk you've taken as a CIO and how did the results turn out?

Shutting down a 3 year ERP project. Results saved the company millions, but cost several executives their positions.
    —*Ray Barnard, Vice President and CIO, Fluor Corporation*

Concluding that a network assessment of a corporate acquisition was inadequate and required an infrastructure overhaul that was done with all network spares sixty hours before going operational. Thirty-six hours of work without replacement by network staff resulted in successful and seamless cutover to users.
    —*Nelson H. Ramos, CIO, IT Strategist, Sutter Health*

WHEN IT MAKES SENSE TO JUMP
TO THE NEXT COMPANY

In the quest for a CIO or technology leadership position, one must assume and take risk and have a demonstrated track record for achievable results. First-time CIOs are hired either from within their existing organization via a promotion, or by another organization, usually via an executive recruiter or a network association. My first CIO opportunity came via another organization at the recommendation of a sitting CIO. I personally know many other IT executives who have experienced both options—internal and external placements. So, when is it necessary or even appropriate to leap to another organization in search of a top IT position? There are several drivers that can lead a person down a path to *jump ship* and look toward another organization for that perfect CIO job. Some examples of when to look at another firm include the following:

- Organizations that are risk-averse with large legacy-based systems and a resistance to change.

- When IT doesn't or no longer has a seat at the management table/committee and is not represented in strategic decisions for the organization. Thus, where IT is viewed as a services or support shop and not as a strategic weapon to help grow the business and support the mission.

- When you're no longer challenged by the projects, assignments, or tasks.

- If a change in senior management and strategy or direction conflicts with your thoughts on where the organization should be going and, more importantly, on how to use technology to get there.

- If you've taken risk(s) that didn't pan out and that negatively impacted your reputation at the firm you're with. If you can repair the reputation inside and desire to stay, go for it; but if the mistake(s) were too great and difficult to recover from and build credibility with other executives and business units, look to another firm and stress the positive accomplishments in your career.

- An obvious one—if you're fired or politely pushed out (hopefully with a package).

- When you've done all you can do and are getting bored, a new challenge and company can be just the right motivator.

- For me—if you're not having fun anymore. I'm a very positive person who works hard and likes to make an impact on the bottom line. If I'm not having fun at it, which could be for a variety of reasons, then it's time to move on and look for another challenging position with a management team and culture that may be a better fit.

- If you're happy with the company you work for and agree with the culture and senior management team strategy, you may want to consider opportunities inside with more responsibility all the way to the office of the CIO. Being happy with your job can mean a lot of different things to different people. According to a *CNN Money* article, Dory Hollander, a career coach, workplace psychologist, and author of *The Doom Loop System*, defines being satisfied with your job if "you can see yourself in three or four years still liking your work, you like the company culture and your coworkers."[13] The *CNN Money* article goes on to describe several other telltale signs that you should start thinking about leaving your current employer:
  - Work doesn't challenge you and you're bored.
  - Things change, and not to your advantage. Examples include negative changes in supervisory reporting or being cut out of the decision-making process.
  - Your boss takes you for granted.
  - Your mood ranges from angry to angrier.[14]

Several readers responded to the *CNN Money* article and wrote in several of their suggestions for when to *jump*:

- When you realize you are more respected outside the company than you are inside the company.

- When you can't think of one thing that you've accomplished in recent times.

- When your boss hires an intern to do a best practices analysis.[15]

According to a *CIO* magazine article, "one of the most challenging aspects of the CIO's career is finding another job."[16] Whether you're looking for a better, more challenging CIO position or that first-time CIO gig, "a job search is about networking, which translates into letting as many people as possible know that you're looking."[17] I asked a group of CIOs their thoughts on giving advice to the next generation of IT leaders. Some of their responses are given below.

CIO SURVEY

What advice would you give midlevel professionals preparing for a CIO role on when to move to the next company?
Make sure that you have some major accomplishments under your belt before you move on. Also, don't burn any bridges with the company you are leaving. It's a small world.
        —*Shyam K. Dunna, CIO/Assistant General Manager, MARTA*
                (Metropolitan Atlanta Rapid Transit Authority)

If your current role does not provide adequate challenge and development opportunity, move when the opportunity within your company is fairly uncertain and you are ready for the challenge.
        —*Jerry B. Hale, CIO and VP Information Technology,*
                Eastman Chemical Company

Understand very well the cognitive preference of the non-IT executive to which you report, whether the CFO or CEO. Make connections with such people, understand at a deeper level their agenda and issues, and aim to provide value to them individually and at the firm level.
        —*Mykolas Rambus, CIO, W.P. Carey*

Was your first CIO appointment from within the company that you were working with?
- 53 percent responded with *yes.*
- 41 percent responded with *no.*
- 6 percent did not respond.

No, however I was being recruited and mentored to become the next CIO at my previous place of business and then an executive recruiter swooped in and convinced me to make the move.
        —*David G. Swartz, VP and CIO, The George Washington University*

WHAT DID I DO TO PREPARE?

Regarding taking risks and risk management, I've had some good mentors in my career who helped me understand what risks are and then develop strategies to manage them. That said, in order to exceed expectations and deliver results consistently, I adopted a *risk-aware* strategy that includes risk management techniques used in conjunction with methodologies and project management best practices. Experience helps develop and refine those skills, which are much needed in the role of the CIO today. I also networked with other IT professionals to learn *best practice* approaches to taking and managing risk.

Regarding whether to look for a CIO position within an existing organization versus going outside, my CIO appointment was via an opportunity in another organization, and the process I went through was fairly straightforward and simple—I was lucky. My career strategy from day 1 has been to (1) continuously develop my professional and technical skills, (2) learn best practices and strategies for managing technology and implementing IT solutions via formal (education) and informal (networking and on the job experience), (3) learn the business of the organization and deliver results to help grow the business and drive operating efficiencies through technology, (4) work hard, (5) reward those that work *smart* and hard, (6) treat others with respect, and (7) continuously raise the bar for myself and my staff. This approach helped me rise through the ranks at a variety of different organizations, gain experience with reputable firms, and develop a portfolio of accomplishments and demonstrated results. The rest was easy—others were willing to go out on their own and recommend me for higher roles of responsibility all the way to when I landed my first CIO position with an international organization at the age of 37. I have no doubt that when I decide to look for that next great opportunity, I'll use every aspect of my professional and personal network to land the perfect position.

RECOMMENDATIONS

To close this chapter, I recommend the following to business and technical professionals seeking results that impact the business and help it grow:

- Learn the business, take *calculated* risks to advance and grow the business, and do your homework on eliminating or minimizing risks associated with projects.

- Research and adopt risk management strategies and techniques.

- Network with peers and other professionals to learn their best practices associated with related projects and strategies and flush out the
  lessons learned to minimize risk. Learning mistakes made by others is
  a great way to avoid making the same mistakes.

- Network with peers and learn their strategies and techniques for
  managing risk

- Build or get on good project teams with solid professional staff that
  gel well together. A good team that is focused on a project is a great
  start to leveraging the right skills for each person, taking risk where
  appropriate, and using risk management strategies.

- On the technology side, conduct technology pilots where appropriate and test new technologies in small scale before deploying them to
  a larger audience.

- Use methodologies and project management best practices in conjunction with risk management strategies to ensure that projects and
  systems implemented match a real business need and are run appropriately and consistently.

- Spend time learning how to do contract management, negotiation,
  and service level agreements. They're critical skills required in today's
  IT field. Leverage vendors appropriately and learn the pros and cons
  associated with the application service provider (ASP) option for
  implementing and hosting systems. According to an IDC survey of
  468 IT professionals, the top five functions most often pushed to an
  ASP include (1) payroll, (2) accounting, (3) intrusion detection,
  (4) web conferencing, and (5) development tools.[18] ASP implementations can also offload the work associated with server management
  and patch management, and can ease disaster recovery labor as well.

- With regard to looking at your current employer versus another one
  for a top IT position, take a pulse on your attitude and happiness
  with your current firm before deciding. If you're thinking positively
  about the culture, management team, direction, and mission well
  into the next several years with your current employer, go for it. If
  you're not happy, challenged, or the culture has changed, start
  preparing to take on a new position of greater responsibility with a
  new firm and sell your best accomplishments to date.

■ ENDNOTES

1. en.thinkexist.com/quotes/t.s._eliot/2.html (accessed August 21, 2005).

2. Scott Berinato, "Risk's Rewards," *CIO* magazine (November 1, 2004), 48.

3. Ibid., 54.

4. Ibid., 50.

5. Ibid.

6. Ibid.

7. Ibid.

8. Ibid.

9. Stephanie Overby, "Bound to Fail," *CIO* magazine (May 1, 2005), 48.

10. Ibid.

11. Ibid., 50.

12. Ibid.

13. Jeanne Sahadi, "Your Job: Signs You've Stayed Too Long," *CNN Money* (July 27, 2005), money.cnn.com/2005/07/26/commentary/everyday/sahadi/index.htm (accessed July 27, 2005).

14. Ibid.

15. Jeanne Sahadi, "Signs You Should Quit Your Job, Part 2," *CNN Money* (August 2, 2005), money.cnn.com/2005/08/02/commentary/everyday/sahadi/index.htm (accessed August 2, 2005).

16. William Crowell, "The Job-Hunting Abyss," *CIO* magazine (August 1, 2002), www.cio.com/archive/080102/peer.html (accessed August 9, 2005).

17. Rob Garretson, "The ASP Reincarnation," *NetworkWorld* magazine (August 29, 2005), 35.

18. Ibid.

CHAPTER 11

The Role of the CIO—
Enabler and Visionary

Flaming enthusiasm, backed by horse sense and persistence, is the quality that most frequently makes for success.[1]

—DALE CARNEGIE

EXPECTATIONS FOR NEW CIOs

So, you've made it to a top IT executive position or have transitioned into another company as an experienced CIO. The CIO role is one of the most demanding jobs in any company and one that usually touches most every employee in one form or another. CIOs today must have a solid resume, a demonstrated set of accomplishments in both areas of technology and supporting and driving the business to new highs, be visionaries that can take an idea and convert it into action, and be able to communicate strategies and wins effectively. Management of the IT function and aligning IT with the business are top functions that CIOs need to pay attention to in the 21st century. According to a *CIO* magazine survey of CIO 100 award recipients in 2003 for resourcefulness, which included CIOs, CTOs, and VPs of IT, respondents indicated the following:

- 73 percent of the CIO 100 awardees have IT organizations that are *centralized* versus decentralized or federated.

- 77 percent manage projects as a *portfolio* as opposed to individually.

- 88 percent have *repeatable processes* (or methodologies) for soliciting new ideas and obtaining funding approval.

- 74 percent share project responsibilities for achieving value with other executives.

- 66 percent frequently or always conduct post implementation audits.

- 95 percent of CIOs reported taking credit for ideas for managing and using IT resourcefully.

- 87 percent indicated that they use *return on investment* (ROI), 59 percent use *total cost of ownership* (TCO), 47 percent use *internal rate of return* (IRR), and 30 percent use an *IT balanced scorecard* to measure IT value.

- 91 percent indicated that *internal customer satisfaction* is most important when determining the value of IT to the business.[2]

What will it take for CIOs to be successful and succeed today and into the future? According to a recent *CIO* magazine article, there are five leadership imperatives for CIOs today:

1. *Drive innovation and growth while managing costs.* While many CEOs want innovation, most CIOs are asked to deliver results that reduce costs. This is one of the most common gaps between CEOs and CIOs today. More on this later in the chapter.

2. *Prove the strategic value of IT.*

3. *Run IT efficiently and effectively.* IT governance is at the heart of running an IT shop efficiently and effectively. A great IT governance program requires knowledge, repeatable processes, standards, and a good defense. Users and sometimes other senior managers don't get that a solid IT governance process can save the organization money. Spend time communicating the why as well as the what.

4. *Develop the next generation of IT leaders.* CIOs are nothing without a good staff—don't forget this! As an adjunct faculty professor for over a decade, I'm a firm believer that you can teach someone something if they want to learn. If the staff that a new CIO inherits has a good

attitude, the desire to learn, and can *become the right stuff*, then develop and enhance their skills. If they can't be developed or don't want to learn, then replace key staff with new staff that *have the right stuff*.

5. *Manage CXO expectations.*[3] One of the most important aspects and challenging tasks of a CIO/CTO is to *understand the expectations* of the CEO, COO, and other key executives. I recommend that CIO candidates spend some time getting the lay of the land during the interview process before taking the IT reigns. Miscommunication between CEOs/COOs and CIOs is a fairly common problem. CIOs that will be successful in the 21st century will (1) make it a top priority to know CEO expectations of the CIO role, (2) learn the business in an effort to align IT to the business and goals, (3) know how they will be measured and evaluated, and (4) think outside the box and not just focus on the IT infrastructure.

A 2003 Forrester Research report goes on to suggest that CIOs also need to develop a *synchronized prioritization* that includes the following:

- *Making IT governance work.* Include other senior executives in the development of the IT governance framework and communicate the *why* frequently.

- *Empower a portfolio management office (PMO) to integrate IT's planning.* The PMO group should own funding, management, and reporting activities for IT investments.

- *Turn cost and impact estimation into core competencies.* With proper research and involvement from other key staff members, CIOs should drive project estimates for budgeting to a reliable and repeatable process.

- *Use metrics to demonstrate prioritization objectivity.*[4] According to Forrester Research, "the top quartile of firms measure 86 percent of their investments."[5]

First-time CIOs are usually hired into senior IT roles that are either new or recently established for growing organizations that have not had a CIO before. That said, not all newly minted first-time CIOs take the helm of a new position. If you're lucky enough to replace a sitting CIO, then you must be well qualified and come to the table with demonstrated skills and accomplishments. *Turnaround* CIOs are almost always very experienced, and are hired for a different reason—to fix an IT department or organization with a significant problem. That said, *turnaround* CIOs require additional skills and prerequisites beyond that of a traditional CIO that include the following:

1. *The ability to deliver quick wins.* For an organization that is struggling, time is money. Find the low-hanging fruit that is causing significant pain and fix it quickly.

2. *Filter the noise.* In an organization with a lot of pain, say an airline in Chapter 11 bankruptcy, there are going to be a lot of problems that may need the attention of the CIO. A good one will quickly employ some risk management techniques and determine what is *noise* and what is *real.* Solve the real problems.

3. *Align IT.* Find out what the business drivers and needs are and focus on IT solutions that meet them first.

4. *Fire and hire right.* Simply put, keep the IT staff that have the best chance of getting quick results and replace the ones that are laggards.

5. *Get the right technology.*[6] Turnaround CIOs can't afford to fail with new or experimental systems and technologies. Thus, they must rely on the best and most proven technologies that can meet the business demand, solve an organizational problem quickly, and have it be supported by the IT staff or appropriate consulting/outsourced partners. The right technology done right will get you closer to recommendation number 1—deliver quick wins.

CIO SURVEY

What are the top five expectations put on CIOs today?
The most common answers are listed below.

1. Learning the business, aligning IT strategies, and *thinking outside of the IT box*
2. Being a change agent for everything that is wrong with the business
3. Using technology to increase profits
4. Reducing costs, improving efficiencies, and meeting financial targets
5. Securing everything

Notables and other interesting and honest comments include the following:

- Having no downtime—ever
- Being able to help the CEO with his or her PC problems (work or home)
- Being infallible
- Meeting demands without proper budgets or adequate IT staff
- Being compliant with regulations (such as Sarbanes-Oxley)
- Ensuring that the technology infrastructure is reliable and available
- Communicating clearly and often

Wow, what a short list! I learned in the first month of my first CIO position that there is no such thing as a top five list. If you want to be a CIO in today's competitive business environment, you'd better get some thick skin, think on your feet, learn the business quickly, and get some results or you'll be out of a job soon.

THE TOP FIVE MISTAKES MOST OFTEN MADE BY CIOs

CIOs, like anyone else, learn by making mistakes themselves or watching others do so. I prefer to learn from a mistake that someone else has made versus one that I've made. Unfortunately, since technology impacts most employees, the tolerance for CIO failure and mistakes is far less than other executive disciplines. That said, the *recipe* for failure for a new CIO is one that can have some pretty bad consequences. I asked my CIO group of experts their opinion on what *not to do*.

CIO SURVEY

What are the top five mistakes most often made by CIOs today?
The most common answers are listed below.

1. Not listening
2. Thinking that the CIO job is mainly technical
3. Not building relationships with key business stakeholders

4. Not communicating what you're doing and why

5. Failing to get business unit or co-executive sponsorship on key business initiatives

This was a great question and one that got far more creative answers than I anticipated. Again, notables include the following:

- Not managing expectations. It's ok to identify key risks and set realistic expectations.
- Not being accountable.
- Lack of imagination.
- Having no IT strategy or vision.
- Caving on IT governance/standards requests.
- Not having a relationship with the CFO.
- Talking techie.
- Chasing new technologies.
- Overpromising and underdelivering.
- Refusing to hire IT staff that are smarter than the CIO.

THE FIRST 100 DAYS—TIPS FROM WORLD-CLASS CIOs

The first 100 days and throughout the first year is a critical time for first-time CIOs and even seasoned CIOs changing jobs. Performance in the first year will likely determine how long the stay at their new company will be. A recent *CIO* magazine article by Martha Heller, managing director of the IT Leadership Practice at the Z Resource Group, offers the following advice to new CIOs that want to survive the first year on the job:

- *Establish your own performance measures.* Work with your supervisor to establish performance measures that are tied to expectations associated with the business.

- *First six months: Ease the easy pain.* Listen to customers and focus on quick wins to establish some credibility.

- *Second six months: Set your agenda.* Develop a longer-term agenda and map a course for the future.

- *Restructure the IT organization (no matter what).*

- *Change behaviors without asking permission.* Take ownership of the IT direction and strategy and press ahead. While feedback from others and peers may seem like a prudent thing to do, don't get too tied up in the process. CIOs are hired to drive the bus and not sit in the back.

- *Track IT spending to earnings before interest, taxes, depreciation, and amortization (EBITDA).* Align IT spending toward initiatives that increase revenue. The CEO's focus is usually to make money. Follow that lead, and use cost cutting where appropriate to assist in reducing expenses and improving the financial picture of the organization.

- *Go for the money.* Go after high-return, low-investment projects first to set the tone with your IT staff and chart a course and attitude that gets IT engaged in the business.

- *Hit the help desk.* Pay attention to your help desk staff and make sure that they're good. This won't necessarily impact the IT bottom line, but will resonate well with your customers that you are customer focused.

- *Hire your own finance manager.* Where appropriate, put someone in charge of integrating with and working with the finance and accounting departments to free you to work and think strategically and tactically as necessary.

- *Ask the business for advice (and write down what people say).*[7] Talk to your customers, at all levels, early in your tenure and write down what they say. Ask for advice and if you act upon it, they'll likely be in your corner in the future.

I've implemented several of these recommendations in my career as a CIO. The one that I disagree with, however, is the recommendation to reorganize the IT department no matter what. If the IT group needs a reorganization, then do it early and in a way that will optimize resources, improve customer service, and increase focus on projects that support the business. If minor adjustments are necessary, take that approach. If the team is working well together and there isn't a real need for a major restructuring, then don't do it. Who knows, maybe the CIO before you got the IT organizational structure right. A restructure that results in reduced performance is not going to benefit anybody. In addition, most reorganizations are stressful on staff and can have significant morale impacts. Thus, my recommendation is to steer the ship to the right course if it needs to be corrected and not mess with it if it doesn't. I asked my group of CIOs their advice on the first 100 days.

CIO SURVEY

What advice would you give *first-time* CIOs to prepare them for their first 100 days on the job?

Many CIOs that I interviewed provided good responses to this question. Some of the best answers and advice are listed below:

- For 30 days, do nothing—except listen. Talk to your staff, customers, vendors, management, and consultants. Review audit management issues; learn the status of systems and new initiatives.
- Days 31–60. Choose who to trust, develop a plan of action based on all you have learned. Carefully share snippets of the plan as you go along, begin to communicate firm parts of the plan, test other parts. Finalize the plan.
- Days 61–90. Share your plan with everyone. Get feedback and modify it. Let your staff know that once the plan is "done" that these will be the marching orders.
- Days 91–100. Share the completed plans with everyone who will listen—vendors, staff, peers, senior management. People can't get behind you if they don't know where you are going. During this whole process, as initiatives in the plan become firm, assign groups to bring the plans into fruition. As of day 100, have a high-level plan that shows the sequence of all the major initiatives and begin to execute and communicate as appropriate. Have FUN—you've worked hard to get here—you are going to work even harder now. And oh yeah—don't be a jerk.

—John R. Sullivan, CIO, AARP

Talk to as many folks as you can concerning opinions and perceptions of your department. For those first few projects, it's better to "under-promise and over-deliver" than to be "late and short."

—Nelson H. Ramos, CIO, IT Strategist, Sutter Health

Know the CEO and CFO expectations. Make sure you have a strong project office. Assess your management team right away. Review all contracts and financial responsibilities you have inherited. Use your

project office to screen the technology chasers. Meet with your customers and listen. Begin your enterprise blueprint and strategy with
an independent third party.

—Earl Monsour, Director, Strategic Information Technologies,
Maricopa Community College District

The first 100 days are easy, you are on the honeymoon. It is the next
100 days that will be the challenge. So, do your best to prepare for
the time ahead. Learn your business and your IT group, build relationships, don't institute radical changes until you have done this.
Look for early demonstrations of your leadership and do not fail!

—David G. Swartz, Vice President and CIO,
The George Washington University

Seek to understand the business and its key components. Meet with
all levels of the organization to understand their requirements, needs,
and issues (both from an IT perspective and overall). Develop a knowledge of the current IT function, its services, strengths and weaknesses, and potential areas of improvement. Be alert to what is and
isn't said in conversations with others—this gives some indication as
to the "true" nature of things. Identify your peer group within the
organization and start to develop business relationships with them.
Identify and if possible, implement a "win" to show that you are taking initiative and are integrating into the organization. Report back to
your superiors and peers on your findings from the first 100 days and
what you see needing to occur in the short- and long-term future.

—Steven W. Agnoli, CIO, Kirkpatrick & Lockhart Nicholson

CEO AND CIO COMMON GAPS
IN EXPECTATIONS

One of the more important things for a CIO to understand in their role is
the expectation of their boss, usually the CEO, COO, or CFO. There can
sometimes be an expectation gap between what the CEO expects of the
CIO and what the CIO interprets as an expectation. Today's CIOs need to
nail these expectations down early in their tenure and be cognizant of what
they will be evaluated on. 7-Eleven's CEO, James Keyes, says, "The role of

IT is to help the company sell more stuff."[8] The *CIO* magazine article featuring Keyes noted that he expected IT to "provide decision support tools for store managers, use technology to deliver new products and services, and pay for new investments through cost savings."[9]

Not all CIOs today, however, get a clear set of expectations from their bosses. Research from Halbrecht Lieberman Associates, who interviewed 25 CEOs and CIOs from Fortune 500 companies, indicated the following gaps between today's CEOs and CIOs:

- Both CEOs and CIOs tended to describe the role of the CIO as *strategic*, but when interviewed in detail, their expectations and realities differed greatly.

- Both CEOs and CIOs agreed in theory that the role of the CIO is one with a focus on being visionary and strategic. When questioned on the detailed activities for CIOs, both responded with roles that were more tactical and operational—keeping the lights on versus driving new product development.[10]

The Halbrecht Lieberman Associates report suggested that there are expectation gaps between CEOs and CIOs and that "CIOs are an untapped arsenal of strategic ideas" while the CIO role is still evolving.[11] In conversations with other CIOs and in my role as a CIO, I have found similar expectation gaps between CEOs and CIOs. Many of us are often asked to think strategically and align IT toward growing the business. In reality, we're often called upon to keep the systems running, grow the infrastructure to support the growth of the business, and make operational cuts and increase efficiencies through technology improvements. Those marching orders are not strategic, but are clearly more operational and tactical at best. So, what are CIOs to do? Should they sit back and wait for the orders to come down? It depends, primarily on the style and preference for communication of the CEO, culture within the organization, and the willingness for CIOs to be reactive versus proactive. Tomorrow's best CIOs will be proactive. It takes work to initiate and get the attention of a CEO, but to be really effective with technology, you need to think strategically and be engaged with the CEO and other business executives who are tasked to drive the business, increase revenue, and grow the organization.

WHAT DID I DO TO PREPARE?

In the first 100 days of my first CIO appointment, I met with a lot of people in the organization at a variety of levels. I asked many questions about how IT was serving the company and solicited feedback from folks I spoke with regarding their perception of IT, any issues, key pain points/problems, and, yes, their recommendations and advice. Once I had a clear picture from our staff and customer base, I had a series of in-depth conversations with the IT staff. Interestingly, there were clear distinct differences between non-IT and IT staff on strategy and perception. Within 30 days I set a course to get some quick wins, and within 45 to 90 days I delivered several improvements and systems enhancements. I started developing my communications strategy with other executives, the CEO, the COO, and my staff. The IT team, augmented with some short-term consultants, delivered some near-term solutions at or under budget, as promised to the COO at the time. It was during the first 100 days or so that I started to develop some credibility with some quick wins and establish some relationships with other senior staff members.

My next task was to (1) get my hands around the budget, (2) slightly modify the structure of the IT group, and (3) develop a long-range IT plan. Over the next several months and years, I implemented the following strategies and changes in an effort to properly align IT with the business:

- Developed a best practice IT governance strategy.
- Developed clear IT policies and procedures.
- Migrated the IT budget from one with *general* budgeting numbers to detailed *line item* numbers by general ledger number and by IT department.
- Defined new IT standards and worked with the IT staff to support and abide by them.
- Developed new change management procedures and deployed a system to document all change requests, detailed migration and rollback procedures, and e-mail-integrated approvals before making changes to production mission-critical systems.
- Developed and deployed methodologies for project justification, requirements, architecture, and implementation.

- Standardized on project management tools and implemented an organizational structure for joint business/IT projects. I mandated that each business unit project would include (1) a project manager in the business unit, (2) an IT lead resource, (3) executive sponsorship and signatories from both IT and the business units, and (4) a signed requirements analysis document before pressing ahead with a solution. The results have been great and have yielded more integrated and enthusiastic business and IT teams.

- Developed relationships with key business unit leaders.

I continue to work with my staff to look for new ways to use technology to help drive the business, deliver results that improve operating efficiencies, and reduce costs. Every day I force myself to think outside of the IT box and never lose site of the goals and challenges of the organization as a whole. Each day that I come home from work I ask myself one simple question—*Did IT add perceived value to the business?* If so, it was a good day. If not, try harder tomorrow.

RECOMMENDATIONS

Whether you're a first-time CIO, a turnaround CIO, or an experienced CIO changing jobs, the task of the CIO is a daunting one that has many ups and downs. I offer the following advice to close out this chapter and book:

- When you're looking for that perfect CIO position, do your homework on the company and try to get a feel for the expectations about the role of the CIO from the CEO. If it matches your expectations and you think that you can succeed, then go for it. If not, walk away and look for a better organizational and potentially cultural fit for your needs and challenges. A challenged, motivated, empowered, and senior management–supported CIO can have a very fulfilling experience and career.

- Be prepared for the interview process, both with the executive recruiter and the employer. I have always treated the interview process as one where we're both interviewing and sizing each other up to ensure a good fit. An interview to me is never a one-sided job interview, but instead a career opportunity.

- Once in the door, listen. Those who act without listening have a fair risk of failure, which may result in a lack of confidence from both the senior management team and your IT staff. Shortly after you start a new position, spend an ample amount of time talking to business customers at a variety of management levels about IT effectiveness and critical issues that may be solved with technology and then bring in your key IT staff members to discuss and strategize on ways to improve where appropriate.

- Get feedback from your IT staff on areas that they think IT does well and areas that they believe could be improved. Take that input along with the business unit feedback and develop a SWOT (Strengths, Weaknesses, Opportunities, and Threats) matrix. I prefer to do this with my key IT staff members as opposed to in a vacuum.

- Shortly after coming on board, review the latest IT audit and put the appropriate resources on tasks that show some clear problems that need a resolution before the next audit.

- Learn the business and develop relationships with key senior management and business unit staff. If you don't understand the key business drivers and challenges, you'll never be able to solve them with technology.

- Develop short- and long-term plans for the IT organization with a focus on IT infrastructure, support, and alignment with the business. Using feedback from conversations along with your SWOT analysis, start laying the framework for an IT roadmap or strategic plan. Work with key IT and business staff to build and refine the plan—starting with a more near-term duration and over time expanding to between 2 and 3 years out. This process will not happen overnight, but is necessary for long-term success and alignment with the business. Where available, adjust the IT strategic plan with input from the organization's business plan or strategy.

- Don't ignore IT best practices. In short, spend enough time focusing on the IT department. Change what needs to be changed and leave what works well alone.

- Talk to IT peers for advice, lessons learned, and best practice implementations. Keep growing your network by integrating and meeting with the *right types* of professionals.

- Communicate effectively up, down, and with peers in the right language. Speak in IT terms to other technologists, in financial terms to the CFO, and in business terms to other nontechnical executives and staff.

- Nail down your budgets and stay focused on meeting or exceeding financial expectations. Oh yeah—try to make friends with the CFO if you want to make your life a little easier.

- Keep your IT staff focused and informed. I frequently run IT all-hands meetings to keep my staff focused on the business at hand and informed on IT strategies, projects, and initiatives.

- Develop a vendor management strategy/framework and over time, look to reduce the number of overall IT vendors supporting the organization. Separate the commodity-based vendors from strategic ones and spend more time building relationships with the ones that provide a strategic impact and value to the organization.

- Keep your IT team challenged and ensure that they have the proper training to perform their duties.

- Have fun. This is a big rule for me. If I'm not enjoying what I'm doing, then I'm in the wrong spot and it's time to move.

- Always make decisions that are in the best interest of the organization and not necessarily for just the IT department.

- Never give up.

ENDNOTES

1. www.famous-quotes-and-quotations.com/success-quotes.html (accessed June 3, 2005).

2. CIO Research Reports, "Best Practices for Resourceful CIOs," *CIO* magazine (August 4, 2003), www2.cio.com/research/surveyreport.cfm?id=60 (accessed August 29, 2003).

3. Edward Prewitt, "What Will It Take for CIOs to Succeed in 2005?" *CIO* magazine (February 1, 2005), 37.

4. Bobby Cameron, Julie Meringer, and Kristin Badowski, "Synchronized Prioritization: A CIO Must-Do" (Cambridge, MA: Forrester Research), December 1, 2003, www.forrester.com/ER/Print/Research/Brief/0,1317,33172,00.html (accessed February 16, 2005).

5. Ibid.

6. Allan Holmes, "Rules of the Road for Turnaround CIOs," *CIO* magazine (August 1, 2005), 58–59.

7. Martha Heller, "Ten Survival Tactics for Your First Year on the Job," *CIO* magazine (September 1, 2005), http://www.cio.com/leadership/buzz/column .html?CID=11451 (accessed September 9, 2005).

8. Christopher Koch, "Who's Mining the Store," *CIO* magazine (May 15, 2005), 52.

9. Ibid., 53.

10. Beverly Lieberman, "CIO—A CEO's Untapped Strategic Arsenal," Halbrecht Lieberman Associates, 11 (unpublished).

11. Ibid.

Index

4